AF425785

This Time I Am Living for HIM

We weren't designed to do life alone

YASMIN ASANTE

This Time I Am Living for Him
By Yasmin Asante
© 2025 Yasmin Asante. All rights reserved.
Published by: Striving for His Excellence LLC
www.strivingforhisexcellence.com
ISBN: 979-8-218-79335-7
Printed in the United States of America

Cover photo by: Jeremy Edwards
Cover design by: Madison Lux
Interior design / Formatting by: Madison Lux
Edited by: Yasmin Asante

This book is a work of nonfiction based on the author's personal experiences and reflections. Any resemblance to actual persons, living or dead, or actual events is purely coincidental unless explicitly stated.

While every effort has been made to ensure accuracy, the author and publisher assume no responsibility for errors, omissions, or changes to content on external websites or resources referenced in this book. Information is provided for educational and inspirational purposes only and should not be considered professional advice. The reader assumes full responsibility for how they use the material.

All Bible verses quoted in this manuscript are taken from the following translations:
New International Version (NIV) © 1973, 1978, 1984, 2011 by Biblica, Inc.
King James Version (KJV) (Public Domain)
Easy-to-Read Version (ERV) © 2006 Bible League International

Note: Additional Bible translations may be referenced throughout the manuscript.

Works Referenced & Influences:
University of Richmond Digital Scholarship Lab, Mapping Inequality Project: Information on federal redlining practices, HOLC maps, and their lasting impact on housing discrimination in the United States. *https://dsl.richmond.edu/panorama/redlining/*
Lisa Nichols: Concepts and quotes from Abundant Life course and motivational speeches.
Pastor Mike Jr.: Quotes from teachings on relationships and self-discovery.
Jekalyn Carr: Reference to the song Greater is Coming.
Yolanda Adams: Reference to the song I'm Gonna Be Ready.
Maranda Curtis: Reference to the song I Am All In.
Tamela Mann: Reference to the song Father, Can You Hear Me?
War Room: Inspiration drawn from the movie directed by Alex Kendrick, written by Alex Kendrick and Stephen Kendrick.
Maya Angelou: Quote: "We delight in the beauty of the butterfly, but rarely admit the changes it has gone through to achieve that beauty."
NAMI: "Kate Spade Suicide | A Note to Loved Ones." June 6, 2018. *https://www.namiccns.org/celebrity-mental-health/kate-spade-suicide-net-worth*

Special thanks to the creators of the Bible translations cited, pastors, historians, motivational speakers, artists, and filmmakers whose works have inspired and enriched this manuscript.

Caution

Content Advisory

This book contains discussions of sensitive topics, including but not limited to loss, grief, trauma, rejection, and emotional healing. While these stories are shared to inspire hope and encourage growth, some readers may find certain sections triggering or emotionally challenging.

If you feel overwhelmed at any point, please take a moment to pause, reflect, and seek support from trusted friends, family, or professionals. Remember, you are not alone, and resources are available to help you navigate difficult emotions.

Support Resources

- Suicide and Crisis Lifeline: Dial 988
- Mental Health Support: Contact a licensed therapist or counselor in your area

This book is intended to offer hope, healing, and encouragement, but your well-being is the priority. Please proceed with care and compassion for yourself.

Dedication

This book is dedicated to my son, Hasaun.

First and foremost, the Lord is my saving grace—but you, my son, have always been the reflection of that grace in my life. The Lord turned my life around so that I could better serve you, and I can only imagine all that He has in store for you.

Keep growing in your relationship with Him—it's the most important one you'll ever have, even above me. He will be the one to lead and direct you on the path He has already predestined for you, to do good works, for you are His masterpiece, created in Christ Jesus –Ephesians 2:10.

He knew you before you were formed in my womb; He chose you and called you –Jeremiah 1:5. He will show you what and who is for you—and who is not. You are a child of the King, and you are deeply important to Him and to His Kingdom.

What an honor it is to be your mom. I love you infinitely and beyond… we both do! (I said it first.)

In Loving Memory

Please take a moment of silence in respect as you read this.

This book is also dedicated to the memory of Antoinette Douglas, whose life and love inspired me in ways words cannot capture. The seeds she sowed continue to nourish not only me but generations. The way she stood in the gap and took up her cross is profound. A great example of what being an ambassador of Christ looks like—not only in her words but in her actions. I can only hope that I too will carry my cross faithfully until the end. We salute you, Queen.

Acknowledgements

Now we ask you, brothers and sisters, to acknowledge those who work hard among you, who care for you in the Lord and who admonish you. –1 Thessalonians 5:12

To Mr. Randy Goodknight, my spiritual father, and to Lady Janelle, my mentor, wise counsel, and sometimes spiritual mom—each of you have poured into my life in such unique and powerful ways.

Mr. Randy, you have known me since I was in seventh grade and have been interceding on my behalf ever since. I can only imagine the late nights and hours the Father may have had you up praying for me—because I was surely something else.

A life laid down you both exemplify; I could never know the cost. Invaluable it is.

Lady Janelle, you literally held me up through it all—the encouragement, the real talks, the prayers, the wisdom, and the love. I will forever cherish them. A true gift indeed.

I'm here because of both of your yes to Jesus. I'm here because you refused to give up. What a gift that our God, our Father, would give unto me. I am a testament of your labor, and "thank you" is not enough. Even in those years when I thought I was all alone and blind to His hand—someone was praying for me.

As Minister Toni would say (aka Antoinette Douglas), "All glory to God, to whom all glory belongs." Amen. Oh, how I pray and hope that my children and loved ones will have a Mr. Randy and a Lady Janelle in their lives—the community leaders, the lady sitting in the church pew, those who truly live and walk for Christ Jesus.

I didn't even know you by the various titles you carry when I first met you, Lady Janelle—just a nice lady at church. I wasn't a churchgoer, so I didn't know the lingo or care for all those additives. I had no idea of the various titles Mr. Randy carried; I just thought he worked for the community center.

I can only hope and pray and strive that I will stay behind the cross, walking in humility with my face set like flint, as long as I live— in Jesus' name. Blooming where I am planted and being about my Father's business.

I am believing for nothing but exceedingly, abundantly more for both of your lives—for your spouses, children, grandchildren, and everyone attached to you. May God continue to prosper you in good health, and may your latter days be far greater than your former.

To my Liberty Baptist family, the intercessory prayer warriors, Ms. Beverly Gordan and Ms. Donna Dase and those He has allowed me to contend with in growing here—again, your labor is not in vain. May the grace and peace of our God continue to fill your lives. May He strengthen you and give you the rest needed as you follow His lead.

I pray that your love may abound more and more in knowledge and depth of insight, so that you may be able to discern what is best and may be pure and blameless for the day of Christ, filled with the fruit of righteousness that comes through Jesus Christ—to the glory and praise of God. –Philippians 1:9–11

As Paul wrote, Pray for me also, that whenever I speak, words may be given me so that I will fearlessly make known the mystery of the gospel… –Ephesians 6:19 Peace and love to all.

Contents

Introduction

You've reached the point in your life where enough is enough. You're tired—and truth be told, you need help. It's just too much. Deep down, you know all will be well, but this time... is different.

For years, I thought I had it all together. I was running, hustling, pushing—until one day, I was completely out of breath.

Imagine a woman in labor, exhausted and in pain. The doctor says, "Just one more push." Despite the agony, she doesn't stop. She pushes through because she knows the joy waiting on the other side. She knows what God has promised her. She's in this thing too deep to turn back.

> She pushes through because she knows the joy waiting on the other side.

So are you.

Just a few more pushes, and you're there.

> Stay in the race.

Life has been a ride for you and yours. But giving up is not an option. Stay in the race. You've been through more than enough. Though it's tough right now, this is not the end. People may have walked out on you. Maybe you've experienced betrayal, loss, disappointment, abandonment, rejection—whatever the case may be. And every time you level up, here comes something else.

But hear me when I say, what you have experienced is nothing compared to what you will gain if you just hold on.

God promises that He has plans to prosper you, not to harm you, but to give you hope and a future. –Jeremiah 29:11.

Victory is already yours. Defeat must bow, depression, lack, fear, doubt, anxiety, sickness, loneliness, and overthinking must bow down in the name of Jesus.

You will make it through.

God did not bring you this far for you to lose. Keep pressing forward! You're closer than you think. You will come out of this, and you will make it through.

So when things feel heavy and you start to question how much more you can take, remember this, the enemy wants you to believe you're alone, that you have no resources, and no one to turn to. The truth is—He will never leave you nor forsake you. –Hebrews 13:5.

You are free. When Jesus died on the cross and rose on the third day—free and victorious—so were you.

Unlearning what you know … step into what is possible.

Walking in that freedom means unlearning what you know to open yourself up to what is true. It requires disrupting what's familiar to step into what is possible.

Just as God knows you intimately, the enemy also studies your patterns and weaknesses. Let's be real though we give the enemy way too much credit. Yes, he is real, but sometimes the issues we face are because of our own bad habits and poor decisions. Which is something we can't fix on our own. You and I can't get ourselves out of this spin cycle. It takes God—and God alone.

Spiritual warfare is very real, and the attacks will come from every direction: our minds, our children, our bodies, our families, our communities, even our neighbors. This is why holding onto God is so important.

Where God is leading you next, you'll need help greater than your own. The old way of saying, "I'll just figure it out," won't work anymore. You made it through before, but now He's calling you higher—to live, not just survive. It's time to build differently. This time, with Him.

I understand what it feels like to be at the end of your rope. I've been there too. I know what it's like to feel alone, to feel like everything is falling apart. But let me tell you—there is hope.

There was a time when, no matter how much good I did, I still found myself struggling. If it wasn't one thing, it was another. A single mom trying to make ends meet, unable to finish my degree, running an organization, building a business—and doors closing on me left and right.

I was honestly beginning to feel the weight of it all. It was too much to bear.

Quite frankly, it was more than juggling those various roles—it was much deeper than I could've known. I couldn't take it anymore. I was tired, gasping for air, and unable to breathe. I was drowning.

But just when I thought it was over, God showed up.

That was a turning point I will never forget. Whenever doubt creeps in (and it does), I look back on that season and remember God's unwavering faithfulness toward me. For God is no respecter of persons. –Acts 10:34. If He did it for me, He will do it for you.

Who This Book is For

Maybe you're a new believer—a sister in Christ—seeking to deepen your faith. Or perhaps you're a tired soul needing reassurance, someone who has tried everything in your own strength and reached a breaking point.

You might be a seasoned woman of God longing to rekindle your relationship with the Father, or simply a curious reader searching for purpose.

Whoever you are, if you're looking for tangible hope, real-life encouragement, and spiritual renewal—I invite you to walk with me through these pages.

The way my life is set up—and how He cleaned me up—I just couldn't keep it to myself.

My hope is that my story will bring you comfort and strength in the middle of your own journey.

How This Book Is Organized

In the pages that follow, I'll walk you through some of the most pivotal seasons of my life. Each chapter focuses on a core faith principle—like learning to trust God in the storm or finding your identity in Christ.

You'll find real-life examples, biblical insights, and practical steps to help you apply the lessons in your own life.

At the end of each chapter, there are reflection questions and journaling prompts to guide you deeper. Whether you're battling feelings of inadequacy, longing to break free from old habits, or simply seeking a fresh start—each chapter is designed to help you embrace the freedom and purpose God has for you.

Working on yourself is one of the hardest journeys you'll ever take. Now is the time to face yourself—and do the work.

After reading this book, my hope is that you will allow God to lead you—and begin to see yourself through His eyes.

No more relying on your own strength. With God as your guide, when you finish reading, may you confidently declare:

"This time, I am living for Him."

CHAPTER ONE

You Cannot Do This by Yourself

Facing the Storm Head On

Repeatedly, you have seen God move in your life. Yet, You talk this big game—"Hallelujah, thank you, Jesus, I trust You, Lord"—but you don't act on it. You're talking the talk but not walking it. Do not merely listen to the word and so deceive yourselves. Do what it says, –James 1:22. If you trust Him as you say you do, then why aren't you taking Him at His word? Why are you living in defeat when you already have the victory?

Before we answer those questions, we need to uncover what's happening inside of us—the doubts, the fears, the worn-out thoughts—that rise up when life feels overwhelming.

Acknowledge the Emotional Toll

Many of us feel like we're on a never-ending treadmill of problems. The moment we overcome one obstacle—here comes something else. It's super annoying. Sometimes it gets to

> Life really does be "life-ing." But God really does be "God-ing."

be so much, you just be like, "I'm done." Here's the truth: our storms are real; life really does be "life-ing." But God really does be "God-ing." He is the same God yesterday, today, and forevermore. Which can be hard to see when you're in the thick of it. But faint not, He will help you in your time of trouble and refuse to give up.

Why Not Give Up?

Because you're still here—and that alone means there's more ahead.

Why not give up? Because there is purpose on your life, even if you can't fully name it yet.

Why not give up? Because you didn't come this far just to turn back now.

Why not give up? Because there are people waiting on you people who need the very thing God placed inside of you.

Why not give up? Because the world needs your light… and I need you too.

I'm not going to hold you though knowing that God is powerful doesn't always stop us from trying to control everything ourselves. I know, because I did it for years and still do at times. I know what it's like to say I "trust God" while still trying to figure out the what, the when, the where and the how. Listen, I be needing to know; okay! Word to the wise all I really need to do is trust Him.

Realizing the True Problem

It took me decades to realize the issue wasn't with God. It wasn't my circumstances or other people—it was me.

One of the hardest truths to accept is that sometimes we are the reason we're stuck.

Not other people. Not the enemy.

Often, it's our own mindset, pride, ego, fears, and insecurities that keep us from moving forward.

Pivotal Moment

Recognizing our own patterns is the first step to growth and maturity. Once we can acknowledge what's been hindering us, we can finally hand those areas over to God—and allow Him to strengthen what has been weak.

Listen, you better believe the enemy has a strategy to take us out. But when we sit down and have the hard conversations with ourselves, that's when things start becoming clear.

We constantly ask God for clarity or breakthrough, but sometimes we aren't willing to do the work. You must do your part—period! That means showing up, being honest with yourself, and with the Lord, allowing Him to craft a new pattern for you

How many times have we blamed everyone and everything else the kids, the dog, the traffic, our jobs, the alarm clock.

As my mom would say, "you give more excuses than the law allows."

When I finally faced the truth that I was part of the problem, I haven't stopped growing since.

Being able to recognize your need to do things differently is major—and I want you to be proud of that.

You wouldn't be who you are today without the storms, hurricanes, and tsunamis you've endured. You were built to last.

You were built to last.

You've trusted so many things and people, giving them chance after chance—yet you hesitate to give God the same honor. We give Him one opportunity. The moment it doesn't work out in our favor, it's "woe is me."

When really, He's the only one who has been faithful. Because as you and I both have experienced, we are human, and sometimes we fail—not only one another, but ourselves.

So what does it really mean to trust? It's more than believing—it's relying, depending fully on the character, ability, and truth of someone. And when it comes to God, He's proven again and again that His character can be trusted.

> Even in the seasons when you didn't call on His name, He was still there.

Take a moment and reflect—not just on the times you called upon the Lord in trouble, and He came through, but also on the moments of peace, joy, provision, and breakthrough where His hand was just as present. Even in the seasons when you didn't call on His name, He was still there.

After reflecting on His faithfulness, can you honestly say He is untrustworthy?

Journaling Prompt

- Write down one moment where God carried you through hardship.
- Write down one moment of joy or celebration where you clearly saw His goodness.
- How do these reminders shape your trust in Him today?

Now think about this: Where have you been placing your trust lately? Have you been leaning fully on God—or on your own ability to manage it all? It's time to stop relying on your own strength and begin trusting the One who created you.

An Overloaded Life

I had piled so much on my own shoulders—full-time student, youth director duties, single motherhood, caregiving, and launching a business. Every day felt like a never-ending checklist, and I thought I could handle it all on my own. I prayed for the blessings and received the blessings—but I wasn't truly including God in the process.

One night, I sat at my desk, trying to finish an assignment before the deadline. My son was calling my name, needing my attention. My phone buzzed—another youth event I had to coordinate. My bank account reminder popped up—another bill due soon. If it wasn't one thing, it was another.

I wanted to cry. I wanted to scream. But instead, I just pushed through—because who else was going to do it? I was exhausted. Even though I prayed for strength, I never actually stopped to listen to what God was trying to tell me. I was moving, but I wasn't hearing Him. I was working, but I wasn't trusting Him. I was on the verge of dropping everything.

To be honest, my relationship with Jesus at that time was more like He was a "Santa Claus." I only went to Him when I needed something. I didn't really know the depth of having a relationship with Him.

I can recall going to church a few times as a kid, but that wasn't really my upbringing. My intentions were good, but looking back, I was not in alignment with His will. Let me tell you—when we don't acknowledge God in all our ways, things will go off course. –Proverbs 3:5 reminds us to trust in the Lord with all our hearts, lean not on our own understanding, and in all our ways acknowledge Him—and He will make our paths straight.

> When we don't acknowledge God in all our ways, things will go off course.

After juggling all those responsibilities, your girl was burnt out.

About ten months into that routine, everything blew up in my face. It was time to return to school for the fall semester, so my job as a caregiver had to end. Out of nowhere, I received a letter stating I couldn't proceed with my final semester unless I paid $10,000.

And then—the woman who owned the building where I planned to host my girls' group cut ties with me a day before the open house. Months of organizing, cleaning, painting, and transforming her space… had me hot.

You know what's dope? When everything was falling apart, I kept seeing rainbows—everywhere I went. Life was life-ing, but God was God-ing, sprinkling hope in the midst of the raging sea. I knew He was speaking to me… even though, at the time, I didn't really understand the significance of the rainbow. I just knew it was bright and beautiful and that joy was going to come.

Now that I know what the rainbow really means—that it's a sign He keeps His promises—every time I see one, I be super geeked! I'm snapping pictures and sending them to everybody I know, lol.

So anyways…

I had poured all my funds into the girls' group and my business, while neglecting my own needs. I hadn't once thought about myself or my son. As a result, my finances were running low, and bills were piling up.

My gas was cut off, and a week after I managed to pay it, my lights were cut off too. That was when I realized: you can be busy doing good things, but if God isn't in it, you can still be out of alignment.

> You can be busy doing good things, but if God isn't in it, you can still be out of alignment.

I was beginning to lose hope, and I desperately needed advice, guidance—something. Up until then, I was used to handling everything alone. That was my norm. Even when I was breaking on the inside, I still showed up like I had it all together.

But this time… I couldn't.

I needed help.

Seeking Wise Counsel

One thing I've learned is this: God never intended for us to navigate life alone.

Where there is no counsel, the people fall; but in the multitude of counselors there is safety. –Proverbs 11:14

The turning point is asking for help. Whether it's a mentor, a pastor, or a therapist… we weren't designed to do life by ourselves.

Sometimes we pray and ask God for answers, but He sends the answer through people. That can be uncomfortable, especially if you've spent most of your life surviving alone. But humility positions us for breakthrough.

Godly Mentors

Whether it's a spiritual father, a spiritual mother, a trusted woman of God, or a Christian counselor, wise counsel can speak truth into our blind spots—the places we can't see clearly.

At that time, I didn't need someone to pity me or tell me what I wanted to hear. I needed someone who would give it to me straight shot no chaser. That's what led me to visit my spiritual father.

I went to see him, and he said, "Yas, you're hurting and need to give up control and pride. God allowed you to have that before, but you must give it back. You can no longer do this in your strength."

When he looked me in the eyes and said those words, I froze. I heard him. I felt the weight of it.

But let go?

How?

I wanted to say, "You don't understand. If I don't do it, who will?"

But the tears welling up told the truth—I was tired.

Bone-deep, soul-wrenching tired.

Then he said, "Soldier up with other folk."

Really? What people?

It had always been just me and my baby boy. Sure, a few people looked out for us here and there, but real support? That was foreign. Where was this so-called community supposed to come from?

Lastly, he said, "Some men will approach you and say the right things to you—EXPECT BETTER."

In that moment, I thought, "If it doesn't apply, let it fly." I believed I was obeying God the whole time, having been celibate for almost two years at the time without entertaining any men. But his words stayed with me, echoing louder than I wanted to admit.

A Moment of Gratitude

Before I go on, I want to say how grateful I am for the people God places in our lives. I am thankful for the mentors and leaders who provide wise counsel and guidance. If you don't have wise counsel, mentors, or therapists—find some, ASAP. Pray about it, and God will bring them to you.

Let me reiterate: We can't do this alone. PERIOD.

Stop Looking for Temporary Fixes

After meeting with my spiritual father, I decided to drive for DoorDash to get my lights turned back on. After dropping off an order, a man approached my car and said, "Excuse me, you know you have a flat tire?" He kindly offered to help.

There I was, standing in the middle of the street, crying, yelling for mercy.

"God, what do You want from me? Help me!"

Right then, the rain started pouring—not a drizzle, but a downpour. I paced back and forth, thoughts racing.

"Man, I should go get high," I thought.

I know it sounds like a scene from a movie, but sis—this really happened. I hadn't smoked in a long time. The crazy part? The guy's friend asked if I wanted to hit the blunt right after I thought it.

I said, "I should… but naw, it's cool. It's not going to do anything for me except ease my mind temporarily."

As soon as the thought came, the offer came—like the enemy was just waiting for me to crack. And for a split second, I almost said yes. I wanted an escape. I wanted something to numb the pain. I had been down that road before, and I knew it would do me no good. So I shook my head and said no.

Sidebar

Notice how quickly temptation showed up right after the thought?

That's why we have to guard our words and thoughts.

James 3:5–6 reminds us:

> Girl, your thoughts and words carry power.

Likewise, the tongue is a small part of the body, but it makes great boasts. Consider what a great forest is set on fire by a small spark. The tongue also is a fire.

Girl, your thoughts and words carry power.

What you entertain—even mentally—can spark an entire chain of events.

This is why we must take every thought captive and make it obedient to Christ.

> But nothing can truly heal us except God.

We often seek temporary relief in our distress—comfort from people, work, food, smoking, drinking… Whatever numbs the moment. But nothing can truly heal us except God.

The guy wasn't able to fix the tire, so he offered to take me to get my son. As we drove, I began sharing what was going on in my life. He was kind… and he was saying all the right things.

Girl, that brotha started looking fine!

At a red light, he leaned over and kissed me.

And yes, I kissed him back.

We picked up my son, and I gave the man my car keys so he could move my car out of someone's garage. He came back that night to return the keys. We made out a little more, and I asked him to stay the night—honestly, I just wanted to be held.

He was respectful and held me just as I asked.

Don't get me wrong, sis—the temptation was real on both sides.

I laid there, crushed by everything happening, and all I could say was,

"Wow… this is how people end up having random sex—because they're vulnerable and just need comfort."

I literally said that out loud.

God was with me—just like He's with you in your struggle.

No amount of sex, liquor, work, or anything else can fix the pain. He is the ultimate Comforter, even when it feels like He isn't there— He is there.

Learning to Receive Help

Later that evening, my sister ChaRae called to check on me. I told her about the flat tire and how I felt like I might end up homeless. She offered to pay to get my lights turned back on, and I immediately said, "Nah, it's cool, sis. I'll figure it out—you have a family to feed."

I instantly rejected help. I don't even think it was pride, but rather a response I'd become used to. When you've spent years doing everything yourself, receiving help feels uncomfortable… even wrong. I had operated like that for nearly a decade. I can only imagine someone who's been operating with that mindset even longer. It's a mentality we must unchain

God does not want you to struggle anymore.

ourselves from. My spiritual father's words echoed in my mind: I had to give that control back.

God does not want you to struggle anymore. He told me to tell you that your struggle is over. We try to figure it out, but He has already worked it out. Just TRUST Him!

You've had chaos, turmoil, and heartache in the past, but God is going to give you peace in the storm this time. Consider this: God is preparing you for a new level. You asked for help—now God is sending it. Be open to receiving it!

The next day, I humbled myself and called my sister for help. Scripture says, Before destruction the heart of man is haughty, and before honor is humility –Proverbs 18:12. I don't believe I was prideful in an arrogant sense—it was more of a natural instinct I had carried for years. Even so, humility meant opening my hands to receive. It wasn't about arrogance; it was about learning to trust God by accepting the help He was sending.

After humbling myself, I realized something important: at one point, you cried because you couldn't do it alone. Now God is giving you the support you need—if you let Him. What I've learned is that we control nothing.

Reflection

What area in your life are you holding onto?
Where do you need to trust God fully? Is it your career,
your relationships, past hurt, or your finances?

I had spent years carrying burdens that weren't mine to carry. Surrender is tricky, and something we must practice constantly—at least if you're anything like me. Chile, I'm forever picking something back up after I laid it at the cross. Crazy work! But here's the truth: when we do lay it in His hands, that's when we receive the help and support we've been longing for. I haven't mastered this, and honestly, God has to remind me constantly to let go and trust Him. But let me tell you—there's real freedom when we do.

> When we do lay it in His hands, that's when we receive the help and support we've been longing for.

MY THOUGHTS

20

$$+$$

CHAPTER TWO

The Prison of the Mind

Freedom Is a State of Mind

Who the Son sets free is free indeed. –John 8:36

Freedom is something we all possess, yet very few of us truly live in it.

I believe that has more to do with a lack of knowing than with simply not caring. We can't live in what we don't know.

Some may argue that Jesus gives us freedom—and He absolutely does. He gives us the freedom to choose: to follow Him or to live by our own means. He's not a forceful God. But let me tell you something: once you get a real taste of what it's like to live for Christ, you won't want to live any other way. Because you've already experienced what it's like to live without Him.

> Once you get a real taste of what it's like to live for Christ, you won't want to live any other way.

What's amazing is, that even those living behind bars can experience a kind of freedom far greater than someone who's never stepped inside a cell—see Acts 16:22–30. I'm not talking about physical liberty; I mean mental, emotional, and spiritual freedom. That kind of freedom only comes from the inside out.

But what if you can't see the bars holding you?

Seeing the Cell Without Bars

One thing about me: I'm a thinker and an analyzer. My momma used to say,

"Girl, you don't get paid to think!"

You hear so much negative talk about overthinkers, but I've come to realize—it's a gift.

Sure, it can be annoying to sit there replaying a conversation I had with Barbara and her dog (yes, even the dog), remembering every word we exchanged.

But hey, that's the way I'm wired.

One day, I was sitting on my couch, staring up at the ceiling, lost in thought, as usual. In that quiet time, the Holy Spirit opened my eyes.

I suddenly saw just how confined and stricken I had been by my past relationships.

Before that moment, God had been showing me an image of a man in a cell. I kept seeing it over and over again, but I didn't fully understand what He was trying to show me.

That day, though—He made it plain.

He revealed that the initials of the three men who had left the deepest imprint on my life spelled out: A.C.J., exactly in that order.

Allegheny County Jail.

Yes, the actual prison located in downtown Pittsburgh, PA.

When I tell you that revelation had me stuck.

Girl, it was like God put language to something I had been living but never defined.

I hadn't been physically locked up, but I had been bound.

Bound in my thoughts. Bound in my emotions.

Bound by the residue of relationships.

Bound in my past.

Your girl was bound.

Shared Struggles, Different Stories

The story I'm telling is mine. It's shaped by my identity, my neighborhood, my culture—But I also know I'm not the only one who's been through it. Pain doesn't discriminate. Trauma doesn't check your race before it enters your house. Mental prisons show up across all communities.

> Mental prisons show up across all communities.

So, while the specifics may change, the spiritual truths remain. And that's why this story matters—because it's not just mine. It's ours.

> This story matters—because it's not just mine. It's ours.

Let that sit for a second.

Mental Prisons Are Inherited, Too

That moment of clarity made me take a deeper look. Not just at them, but at myself.

At first, the thought of a mental prison never crossed my mind.

For the record, these men were never physically in jail. But they were locked up in other ways. They were shaped by culture, music, survival, and the environment around them. So was I.

Don't get me wrong—they were good men.

They were simply doing the best they could to "make it" in a world that offered them limited choices.

Sometimes, they're built from beliefs we were handed, patterns we never questioned, or trauma we never processed.

It reminds me of Jesus's words in John 17:16—that we are not of this world, even though we live in it. Unfortunately, when we don't know who we are or where we come from, we start living like we belong to the very systems we've been called to rise above. And that's the thing about mental prisons, they're not always obvious. They aren't always the result of poor choices. Sometimes, they're built from beliefs we were handed, patterns we never questioned, or trauma we never processed.

Mental bondage doesn't always begin with us. Sometimes, it's inherited—passed down through generations. We hear things like, "I don't need nobody," or "you don't need a man to take care of you," and without realizing it, we build our cells with those words. Carried in the language of the streets, the silence of our households, and the norms of our communities. The world around us has a way of shaping our internal walls before we even know we're building them.

Reflect for a moment

What unseen chains might you be carrying?

Historical Context: The Redlining Factor

When I think about why so many of us have been stuck mentally, I can't help but point to systems that were never built for us to thrive in. One that stands out the most? Redlining.

We were taken out of thriving neighborhoods—places where we once owned businesses, raised children, and built community. We weren't just relocated—we were restricted. Stripped of resources, denied opportunity, and confined to survive in desolate places.

I'm talking about neighborhoods with liquor stores on every corner, and abandoned buildings.

Places where hope felt scarce, and survival became the focus.

This didn't just happen. It was strategic.

Back in the 1930s, the federal government created residential security maps through the Homeowners' Loan Corporation (HOLC). These maps literally graded neighborhoods by risk—and any area that was predominantly Black was marked in red, labeled hazardous, and denied investment. This is what is known as redlining. Research from the University of Richmond's Mapping Inequality project shows that these maps had long-term consequences, denying families access to loans, insurance, and the opportunity to build wealth through homeownership.

So, while Black communities in the early 20th century—especially during the Harlem Renaissance and the decades that followed—were innovating, creating, and thriving, redlining intentionally stifled that growth. It relocated us into underserved areas and called it housing assistance.

We're still living with the ripple effects today. Many of us don't even realize how deeply our environments shaped the way we think, love, and operate. That is how mental prisons get built—through restriction, through survival mode, through watching our parents and grandparents do what they had to do without space to heal.

Unlearning Generations of Bondage

Although we're free, we have much to unlearn. It won't happen overnight. We must unlearn how we think, speak, dress, operate. We function in this world, but it's not our home. Instead of craving its treasures, ask God to help unlearn ignorance and teach you how to move—because if you have accepted Christ into your life, then the Holy Spirit lives within you and, baby, you are free.

> It won't happen overnight.

Deuteronomy 7:7-9

The Lord didn't choose you because you were numerous; you were few. But because He loved you and kept His oath to your ancestors, He brought you out of slavery with a mighty hand. He's faithful, keeping His covenant of love for those who love Him.

> Freedom is a gift we already have—not something we have to find.

Our true freedom comes at a price. Let's use the gifts He's given us for His glory and to love His children. Freedom is a gift we already have—not something we have to find. Ask the Lord what to do with this newfound freedom.

What good is it for someone to gain the whole world, yet forfeit their soul? –Mark 8:36

We like to forget about our history and move toward the future. However, to move forward, we must start with the root. These systems didn't just steal opportunities—they stole lives. Even more painfully, they shaped how we saw ourselves.

> To move forward, we must start with the root.

Pause and ask yourself

How has your environment shaped not just where you live, but how you see the world—and yourself?

Young Lives Lost and Unhealed Wounds

It wasn't just the environment that shaped me—it was the people.

Those surroundings, those systems, those unspoken expectations they all had faces.

For me, they looked like A, C, and J. Each of them carried stories shaped by the world we came from.

Two of the men I speak of—A and C—had their lives tragically cut short at just 24 and 25 years old. Two young men, gone too soon. Their loss sent a ripple of grief, leaving indescribable pain and emptiness among their loved ones. And for what? Absolutely nothing—just senseless. Yet, unfortunately, we continue to hurt one another, causing pain that could be avoided. We need love. Where is the love?

Pause for a moment

How has loss shaped the way you trust or love?

Entering a New Chapter: J

While the losses of A and C left their mark on my heart, I was still navigating my own unhealed spaces when J came into my life. At the time, I wasn't ready for any kind of relationship—I hadn't healed from the past, and honestly, I didn't even know how. As a result, I was plain old mean to J. I was just too numb by the time he came into the picture.

My Hands Weren't Clean Either

Looking back, I realized my heartbreak wasn't just about what happened to them—it was about what was happening in me.

> We, as women, can sometimes blame men for how they treat us.

From my experience, I've noticed that we, as women, can sometimes blame men for how they treat us. We say, "That ninja ain't—" you know the rest. The reality, though, is that we allow it. When we don't know our worth, we tolerate any and everything. I know I did. I'm convinced that when people say, "You deserve better," it's not always about a better man—it's about becoming a better you. The

> When we don't know our worth, we tolerate any and everything.

way we allow men to treat us is a reflection not only of what we believe we deserve, but also of how we treat ourselves.

Instead of blaming the fellas, place a demand on yourself. And after placing that demand, turn within and begin to build; not toward a man, but within your own soul. Because if you don't begin to value yourself, then why should anyone else?

Jumping from relationship to relationship ain't it. Take the real time to heal. Get to know you. How you really get to know you is by getting to know Christ. We go deeper into this later. That's the only way you'll truly grow.

> How you really get to know you is by getting to know Christ.

Healing from Early Trauma

That healing I mentioned? It isn't just about moving on from a breakup. It's about breaking free from the prisons we didn't even realize we were living in.

For me, one of those prisons was built in my teenage years, when I experienced the loss of my son's father (A). That kind of trauma doesn't just hurt—it shapes how you think, how you trust, how you survive. Let me take you back.

I was 17 years old when I got pregnant and 18 when I had my son. Of course, my family wasn't thrilled. An interesting pregnancy, to say the least. One month before I had my son, I had to leave my mom's house. At the time, it felt like rejection, and I had to figure out how to survive on my own. I wouldn't be the woman I am today had it been any different. Just three months after having my baby boy, we lost his father. I was torn up—broken, lost, depressed, and hopeless. I had no idea what I was going to do. I was a baby raising a baby, grieving, and feeling completely alone.

It wasn't totally over me though. God always comes to my rescue—always. Even when I didn't know it. My big cousin let my newborn son and me stay with him and his three kids. My "mom-in-love," Charece, would try to talk to me about God.

> Little did I know she was planting seeds

Every time she did, I didn't want to hear it. Little did I know she was planting seeds –1 Corinthians 3:6–8. At that time, I didn't believe God was even real. How could a loving God deal me a hand like that? I started smoking Black & Milds and weed daily, barely ate, and rarely left the attic.

After about six months, my cousin said,

"Yas, I love you and my lil cuz, and you can stay as long as you need. But ain't nobody going to love that baby or give him what he needs but you."

That was all I needed to hear.

Reflect

What "wake-up call" have you received that reminded you that you needed to get your act together?

The Mask of Strength

Three months after my cousin sat me down, I moved into a place in the McKeesport projects, started paralegal school, and worked as an administrative assistant. On the outside, it looked like I had it together—but behind closed doors, it was far from pretty. I smiled in public, but inside? I was shot out. I told people I was "okay" when I was barely holding myself together.

I felt like I had to prove myself.

I played the role of the strong woman, but inside? I was breaking. The worst part? I couldn't see beyond my circumstances. I had convinced myself that if I looked good, I was good. But that was just a mask. Without the support I wanted—and thought I needed—I felt like I had to prove myself: that I could make it on my own, that I wasn't just another statistic. That's the thing about a mental prison—it convinces you to stay in places you were only meant to grow from.

Reflect

What mask have you been wearing just to make it through?
What would it look like to finally lay it down?

Each layer of pain I didn't process became another brick in the prison I was unknowingly building around my heart. The more I avoided what was underneath, the more I attracted situations that matched my brokenness.

That's when I met C. He was a business major, and I practically worshipped the ground he walked on. If he said "jump," I said, "how high?" Crazy, I know. That relationship pulled me deeper into darkness. That's when I started smoking cigarettes, popping pills, and drinking lean. He'd come home at wild hours, call me out of my name, and entertain other women. Still, I played the "ride-or-die."

I didn't want my son to grow up without a two-parent home. So, I accepted what I accepted. The way I was moving, my son could've ended up in the system, and I could've lost my mind on drugs— or worse. That still makes me quiver to this day.

The Breaking Point

I trusted no one. To get by, I started stealing from stores. This was a little before I got the administrative assistant job. I was receiving a small welfare check, around $150 in cash at the time. It didn't stretch far, and with the way I was coping, I wasn't thinking about making it stretch. I was reckless and lost.

One day, I was strolling my son through the store, tucking things into the stroller, and got caught. Blessedly, the store owner let me off with a warning. God was watching out for me yet again.

Eventually, C and I went our separate ways. It was painful, but necessary. Even though I didn't leave fully healed, I left. Walking away was the first step toward breaking free from that mental prison.

A Chance for Forgiveness

A few months after C and I broke up, I met someone new—J. At first, I wasn't attracted to him. J was nothing like C. He had something different: consistency and compassion. Most of all, he genuinely cared—not just about me, but about my son. That's what began to pique my interest in him.

As I was beginning to move on from C and trying to rebuild, I moved into a new home with my son. Life was still messy, but I was doing my best to push forward. J and I were growing closer. Then, just two months after moving in, I got a late-night call from C. He was hysterical. I could hear the fear in his voice, so I invited him over.

He showed up shaken. It felt like one of those movie moments where someone goes to the priest to confess everything before it's too late. He poured out his heart, sharing things I've never repeated to this day—secrets, regrets, fears. It was heavy.

Over the next two weeks, we reconnected—not romantically, but in a real, honest way. He apologized for everything. "I should've married you. Been kissing your feet," he said. "Now you know what not to look for." Where was this man before? I wondered.

I loved seeing C turn over a new leaf. He even washed his white clothes at my house. But J was coming over the next day, and I didn't want to send the wrong message. So I told C he needed to come pick his stuff up. That was the last time I saw him.

Before he left, we joked a bit. He teased me about J, saying, "That's not going to last." Then he said, "If anything happens, watch out for my mom." I waved it off with a smile. "Boy, please. Nothing's going to happen to you." I gave him a hug. But something about that moment felt different.

After closing the door, I walked to the window to watch him walk off. He turned, and we just... stared. My hand was still on the curtain as we waved our goodbyes. I knew it was a final goodbye; I just didn't know it was *thee* final goodbye. The day after my 22nd birthday, C was taken. Another trauma added to the mental prison I was still trapped in. That's when I really noticed God reaching out to me.

> That's when I really noticed God reaching out to me.

First Encounter With God

I grieved C differently than I did A. While I didn't spiral as far this time—maybe because I was in a relationship with J—I still hadn't fully processed the pain. I was holding so much inside, and I wasn't exactly kind to J. As I mentioned before, I was mean, distant, and wrapped up in my own hurt.

Just two weeks after C's death on June 3rd, I had a moment that changed everything: my first real encounter with God. We went on a family vacation to an indoor water park, Kalahari. I was getting high on the balcony with my siblings when I noticed something strange:

a tree in the distance that seemed to form the shape of a right hand. In the palm was a book, illuminated by bright light, and on the index finger was a cross.

At first, I thought my mind was playing tricks on me. But when I asked my brother and sister if they saw it too, I knew I wasn't imagining things. My brother couldn't see it at first, so I told him to look closer. He playfully said, "Eww, get away from me. You're one of those people," and jokingly added, "Yeah, I ain't messing with you."

After witnessing that, I suddenly felt the urge to lay down in bed. As I scrolled through my Facebook feed, a video caught my attention. I can't remember exactly what it said, but amidst the whispers I thought I heard from my siblings, I could feel something shifting inside me. Mind you, I was high as a kite—but fully alert. The next thing I knew, I began talking to God. As soon as I did, the video stopped instantly. I fell to my knees, and for the first time in my life, I began to genuinely repent. That was the very first time I prayed like that. From that moment on, I began noticing scriptures everywhere— on billboard signs, passing cars, even random places in the city. God's word was there, constantly.

Reflect

Think about your first real encounter with God.
What do you remember about that moment? How
did it shape your faith or life journey?

From Pre-Faith to Post-Faith

Months later, I went to church with my grandma, who had been patiently praying to see one of her seeds come to Christ. Every time she invited me before, I had a list of reasons why I wasn't ready. "I gotta stop cussing first," I'd say. "I need to get myself together." But Grandma would just smile and say, "Yassy, I hear you. But God will take care of that."

Stepping Out

When the pastor invited anyone who wanted to give their life to Christ, I stood up. Grandma, whose leg had been in so much pain, suddenly was healed. Y'all, she bolted down the aisle as I accepted Christ. That pain was gone. Her leg said, "Pain? Where?" lol.

Here's the thing: I didn't really feel anything at that moment. No tears, no emotional outburst. I just stood there. Everyone was clapping, hugging me, congratulating me, but inside, I felt blank. It wasn't dramatic. I wasn't overwhelmed, and I didn't hear God's voice or feel some holy electricity shoot through my body like we all imagine it to be, lol.

That couldn't be further from the truth.

Looking back, I didn't fully understand what I was doing I just knew I needed to do it. I didn't have to feel "ready" or be emotionally moved to say yes. I just had to say yes.

Grandma was right. We often think we need to have our lives together before accepting Christ. That couldn't be further from the truth.

I was speaking to a reverend one day, and we discussed this exact mindset: Where does the idea come from that we must "get ourselves together" before coming to Christ? From his perspective, as a baby boomer who grew up in

We got comfortable preaching breakthroughs but avoided the long-suffering that often comes before it.

the church, it stems from the masks people wear. Somewhere along the way, we stopped being vulnerable. We stopped testifying about our defeats and started only sharing the "feel good" parts of faith. We got comfortable preaching breakthroughs but avoided the long-suffering that often comes before it. That perspective stuck with me—and I thought it was worth sharing.

> God meets us right where we are.

This mindset that we must clean ourselves up first? It's a trap. It will keep us waiting a lifetime. Just like Grandma and the reverend said: God meets us right where we are. Once we accept Him, those addictions and bad habits begin to lose their grip. It's a process—but God wants us, mess and all.

The Bible isn't a rule book—it's a love letter. He meets us where we are, even in the darkest, craziest places of our lives. He never asked for perfection. He asked for you—broken, beautiful you.

> He never asked for perfection. He asked for you–broken, beautiful you.

When I truly began seeking Him and surrendering my plans, I realized that real freedom doesn't come from being in control. It comes from letting go of the mental prisons I had built.

Freedom doesn't mean life stops hurting. It means you're free to heal, to rest, and to become who God created you to be—before the world tried to tell you otherwise.

We wear strength like armor while dying inside. But it's in our brokenness—in our mess—that God shows up.

Mini-Reflection

What definition of freedom have you been taught?

The Tragic Example of Kate Spade

Sometimes, the chains we face aren't visible to others. You never really know the battles someone is fighting behind the scenes. I was reminded of this when I heard about Kate Spade—yes, the iconic designer and founder of Kate Spade New York. She built a global fashion brand. Her net worth was reportedly over $200 million. By the world's standards, she had everything. But in 2018, Kate took her own life after a battle with depression. All that wealth, all that success—and still, she was stuck in a mental prison. Her story hit close to home for me.

I wasn't having suicidal thoughts, but I knew what it meant to wear a mask and suffer in silence. One day, I was at a family cookout. It might've been around the time C was murdered. I was tore up—and it did not look good on me. Everyone was laughing and joking, and I was just… there. Not one person came up and asked if I was okay. Maybe my family was wearing their own masks and couldn't see mine. Who knows? But I'll say this: if you ever notice irregular behavior from someone you love, pause. Look past the surface. Ask them if they're okay—genuinely. It's not always someone "trying to be grown" or "being disrespectful."

Pain doesn't always announce itself loudly. Sometimes it looks like a quiet smile. Trauma, depression, and suicidal thoughts are real. If that's you or someone you know, please seek help. Talk to a therapist. Tell your doctor. And if you're in crisis, call 988—the Suicide and Crisis Lifeline. Prayer is essential. God will meet you where you are, with no shame and no guilt. But sometimes, He'll meet you through a professional. Which is also needed.

The Pain of Loss

It wasn't just the grief of losing A and C; it was deeper than that. It was the ache of feeling like my family wasn't truly in my corner. It was the weight of trying to hold everything together as a single mother. It was all of it—stacked, layered, and unspoken.

Now, I'll be honest: I wasn't terrible, but I wasn't an angel either. I'm the youngest of my mother's four children, and she raised us as a single mom from the time I was 10. If you ask her, she'll tell you I'm the one who gave her the most trouble.

They say it takes a village to raise a child—but in my eyes, my mom didn't have one. She was out here doing the best she could with what she knew, with what she had. And for that, I honor her now. But then? I didn't understand.

Looking back, I realize—I could've lost my mind. I should've lost my mind. But God. That pain taught me, but it didn't define me. Yet here I am, still standing, even with the storm still raging some days. And because I've come through, I know we have work to do. As Haggai 2:4 says, But now be strong, Zerubbabel,' declares the LORD. 'Be strong, Joshua son of Jozadak, the high priest. Be strong, all you people of the land,' declares the LORD, 'and work. For I am with you,' declares the LORD Almighty.

Final Thoughts: Breaking Mental Prisons Through Faith

The mind can be its own prison, but faith in God breaks every chain. You—the one still pushing through despite pain and setbacks—you are part of the answer. Maybe the lessons you've learned, the endurance you've built, the heart you've cultivated through grief... maybe that's your blueprint for someone else's freedom. Embrace the freedom He's already given you—freedom to heal, forgive, grow and rest. Allow Him to transform your mind and your life.

> The mind can be its own prison,
> but faith in God breaks every chain.

MY THOUGHTS

CHAPTER THREE

Shifting the Mind

"The mind is a terrible thing to waste but a wonderful thing to invest in." –UNCF

We've already talked about how trauma—whether generational, environmental, or personal—can trap us mentally. But I want to highlight something just as real: you can adopt a whole new mindset, completely different from the one you were taught.

When we take time to invest in our minds, we begin to unlock what once felt impossible. Whether we realize it or not, we're investing in our minds every single day—through what we watch, what we read, who we listen to, and who we allow into our inner circle.

The question is: **What are you feeding it?**

"Everything starts and ends in your mind. What you give power to has power over you, if you allow it." –Les Brown

For example, if you keep telling yourself, "I'll never make it to the other side, I'll never amount to anything," then let me be real with you—you're right. But if you tell yourself, "I'm going to get to the other side, no matter what. I'm crossing that finish line, baby!"— guess what? You're right again. As Proverbs 23:7 (KJV) says, For as he thinketh in his heart, so is he. If you think you can, you're right. If you think you can't, you're right.

As you grow, as you mature, it becomes vital to start being intentional with how you invest your time and energy. Let me take you to a moment in my life—the exact point when the way I thought about myself, the way I saw myself, began to shift.

Summer 2016: Personal Breakthrough

One day, my little cousin shared this YouTube video about rewiring your mindset. Y'all, it was everything—so inspiring, so encouraging, exactly what I needed at that moment. At the time, I was still grieving and mourning C. I must have watched that video a dozen times, just letting it sink in.

That's how I discovered Lisa Nichols, a bestselling author and motivational speaker who had once been on welfare. She was a Black single mom of a baby boy, and now she was out here helping other women like me get back up. I was in awe of her—because she looked like me and had been through some of the same struggles. When she spoke, it felt like a big sister was right there, pouring life into me.

If she could overcome the odds stacked against her, then maybe— just maybe—I could too. She gave me hope and affirmed what I'd already been telling myself after having my son: I was more than just a statistic.

When I found out Lisa Nichols would be hosting a conference in Chicago, I just knew I had to be there. It's one thing to watch online, to listen from afar—but there's nothing like an in-person connection. And baby, I was going to be there no matter what—even if my family didn't understand.

"Women shouldn't travel alone."

"You can motivate yourself."

"You don't have enough money."

That's what they kept saying. They didn't realize how badly I needed this. I believed if I went to that conference, it would change everything—not just for me, but for my whole family. I don't know, but I've always had this sense of "make a difference," this "there's more for us" kind of mentality—ever since I was a little girl.

> Stop seeking validation and move with God.

So, with just $56 in my pocket, I left home on a mission.

Stop seeking validation and move with God.

Let me make something clear to you, sis: everyone won't understand your walk, and that's okay. "What God gave you was between you and Him—it wasn't a conference call". Period.

A lot of us don't step out and make our dreams happen because we're too busy listening to what others say won't work. Which is wild—like, how are you going to ask somebody who's never opened a restaurant how to open one?

And then, when you don't get the answer you were hoping for, you've got the nerve to call it hating. Sis, they're not hating on you— they just don't know. That's why we've got to take it to God first, and then trust Him to send us the who and the what we need.

The Journey to Chicago

When I arrived at the Pittsburgh airport, my flight was delayed by six hours. Mind you, this was my first time flying, so of course I was nervous, wondering if maybe it was a sign I shouldn't go. Then I remembered—my phone bill was due, and I hadn't paid it yet. It wouldn't be me otherwise, right? My momma always said I came out backwards, lol.

I went back and forth about calling my dad because I already knew I was gonna hear it. But I swallowed my pride and called him—I didn't really have a choice anyway. Truth is, he wasn't feeling me going on the trip from jump. Not because he didn't care, but because he wanted me safe. I just couldn't see that then.

I realize now that when my family reacted the way they did, they may not have fully understood me, but nonetheless, it was their way of showing love and care. Love shows up in so many forms—not always the way we expect it, or even in the way we know how to express it ourselves.

> Sometimes we miss love because we only see it through our own lens.

Sometimes we miss love because we only see it through our own lens. We want it to sound a certain way, look how we think it should, or act like we would act. And when it doesn't, we brush it off. But love doesn't always show up how we expect—it often comes in ways we don't recognize until later.

For example, just because I might yell at you for wearing a half-shirt and short shorts doesn't mean I don't think you're beautiful or that I don't want you to live your life. It means I love you and don't want men to objectify you when you are more precious than rubies.

Or maybe I don't say, "I love you," out loud, but I show up for you every single time—that's love too. Some people didn't grow up hearing those words, so instead of saying them, they learned to show love through their actions.

And wouldn't you know it? Right after my dad paid my phone bill, my plane arrived. Talk about divine timing.

I landed in Chicago around 2 a.m. I thought I would catch a jitney upon arrival—if you aren't familiar with the term, a jitney is basically an affordable taxi. So, I just knew Chicago would be like Pittsburgh in that sense. I was thinking, Okay, a quick $15–$20 trip—easy.

Your girl was all the way wrong.

I ended up needing a cab instead. The ride cost $84—and I only had $56. (Exactly what my people had been warning me about.) Fortunately, the driver turned off the meter and took what I had. "Wont He do it"!

Listen—the earth is the Lord's and the fullness thereof. –Psalm 24:1

My Daddy owns the cattle on a thousand hills. –Psalm 50:10

I checked in with my grandma who was keeping my son and she stayed on the phone with me the whole time until I got to the hotel safely. That's really my girl, her prayers kept me—still keep me—and cover our family.

When I look at my bloodline, my grandmother—my father's mother—is the only believer I knew of growing up. When I tell her that, she always says, "Oh, Yassy, you come from women who could pray. Women who were about the Lord." She'll tell me that her grandmothers are the ones who raised her and taught her about God.

Generational Blessings

We don't talk about it enough, but generational blessings are real. The doors we walk through today—many of them were opened by the blood, sweat, tears, and prayers of those who came before us. We're literally standing on the backs of some soldiers.

We need to learn to honor them, especially while they're still alive and well. Check on them. Make sure they're okay. Cook them a meal, send a card—nothing major. Just let them know you care and that they matter. A little really does go a long way.

And trust me, sis, I'm talking to myself too.

I never got to meet the women my grandmother spoke of, but I know I am living in the fruit of their prayers. How powerful is that? Some of the favor we walk in isn't because of what we've done—but because of what they planted, what they carried, and their refusal to give up and to keep believing in the one true, living King.

The same God who spoke to Moses, who was with Joshua and Mary, is the same God who spoke to our grandmothers, mothers, fathers, leaders and mentors—and the same God we get to commune with now.

A Divine Encounter

I arrived at the hotel around 4 a.m. and only managed to get a little sleep before the event started at 9. When I checked Google Maps, I realized the venue was two hours away.

As I got ready, I noticed the sky was cloudy and gray which was surprising, given the forecast in Pittsburgh had called for sunshine. I didn't pack extra clothes given this was my first time traveling. After showering, I put my travel clothes back on. As I decided I would just change into my dress and heels once I got to the Abundance Now event. Before heading out, I asked the front desk receptionist if they had an umbrella. Thankfully, she offered me hers. With gospel playing—and a little bit of that good ole R&B in my ears—I was headed towards my breakthrough.

About 15 minutes from the venue, my GPS started going in circles. Mind you this is early morning now and most stores were closed. I saw a Family Dollar and began walking toward it, hoping to get my bearings.

Suddenly, a man in a red van pulled up and asked if I needed help. I could tell he'd seen the worry written all over me. Without hesitation, he offered me a ride. "I asked that man was he going to take me straight to my destination".

He said yes. I was so desperate for a breakthrough that I jumped right in. Never even thinking about the potential danger. Thank God he was cool! But girl, let me just say this—do not do what I did, okay? During the ride, he told me about his family and asked what brought me to Chicago? I shared my story. he listened, but still said, "You don't need a coach, You can motivate yourself."

He sounded just like my family back home. Despite my attempts to explain how much this meant to me, he didn't quite get it. But before I got out, he said, "Alright, lil sis, go ahead and make us proud."

When we pulled up to the venue, the sun was shining like it had never rained. It felt like a movie. I had just walked for nearly two hours in the pouring rain, yet the sky was now clear and bright. I can't make this stuff up!

Everyone there looked beautiful, and I stood there looking like, "Who did it and why?"

Embarrassed, I signed in and rushed to the restroom to change. I pulled out my light pink dress, feeling relieved—until I saw blue ink stains all over it from being stuffed in my bag.

At that point, it felt like if it wasn't one thing, it was another. I broke down and sobbed; Like, full on ugly cry.

That's when a mother and daughter noticed me and stopped to console me. I shared the journey I had just traveled on, and they reassured me that all was well and helped me see that, despite everything—I had made it.

Just when I was feeling discouraged, He swooped right in. He is a mother to the motherless, for sure.

They comforted and affirmed me. Then, with gentleness, they asked, 'Did you bring food today?'"

> "God isn't checking your bank account—He wants to see how much faith you have?"

I hadn't even thought about eating. I just knew I needed to be in that room.

Their response? "Let us pay for your meal."

Jesus! You ever hear the saying; "God isn't checking your bank account—He wants to see how much faith you have?"

My God shall supply all your needs according to His riches in glory. –Philippians 4:19

He is a Comforter, a Healer, a Way maker, my shelter, a Mighty Protector, a mother, a Father, and a Friend. He is everything you need—when you need it.

Hallelujah Glory to God to whom all Glory belongs to!

To put the icing on the cake? Lisa Nichols' niece overheard my conversation with the mother-daughter duo and arranged for me to have a one-on-one meeting with Lisa herself, along with a photo.

Talk about exceedingly, abundantly above all you can ask or think. –Ephesians 3:20

Despite all the chaos, it turned out to be one of my best trips ever; a room filled with positivity, joy, love, and laughter. It was exactly what I needed. Especially after the storms, hurricanes and tsunamis I mentioned in the earlier chapters. A room full of possibilities.

Since then, I've attended even more daring and inspiring conferences—willing to take big risks just to become a better version of myself. Because the one I was given, my son, didn't ask to be here, and I was determined to give him more.

I didn't have it all figured out, but I knew there had to be more—for me, for us. And that more eventually grew into a more for all of us.

Reflection

Are you willing to take a risk?
If God said "move" today, would you go?
Or would you need more convincing?
How deep is your faith?
Where have you been hesitating, even
though your spirit knows it's time?

True Transformation: The Power of God's Word

Since the Abundance Now conference in 2017, I started intentionally filling myself up and surrounding myself with positivity. Personal development became part of who I was—and still is. I made a choice to delete all forms of negativity from my world.

You know that line we say when we're trying to grow? "I'm not talking to anybody right now—I need to work on me and get myself together."

So you pause on dating. You start drinking more water, exercising, listening to uplifting music, watching inspirational videos. You know how it is when you're hungry for more. That was my routine every time I wanted to change or evolve.

I posted affirmations everywhere—on my walls, my son's walls, car mirrors, in the bathroom. I made sure I looked good, took my bubble baths, and even started dating myself. I felt different. I knew I was different. I was determined to help other women love themselves too.

But eventually, I found myself in a cycle. I couldn't understand it. I was doing the work—so why did I still feel stuck?

Granted, my desires were changing. My thinking was shifting. I was leaning into healthier habits—but it still wasn't taking root.

Well without the Word of God, all that positive thinking was just surface-level.

Man shall not live on bread alone, but by every word that comes from the mouth of God. –Matthew 4:4

The world will tell you to "put yourself first" and "love yourself."

Well, that's not totally wrong—I do believe you should love yourself. But putting yourself first is how we keep ending up in those cycles we talked about. God is to be first—not just before the people in our lives, but above you as well.

How can we truly love ourselves if we don't even know what love is? You can't love yourself fully until you know God—because He is love. A relationship with God is also a relationship with yourself.

Love the Lord your God with all your heart, all your soul, and all your strength. These commandments that I give you today are to be on your hearts. Impress them on your children. Talk about them when you sit at home and when you walk along the road, when you lie down and when you get up. Tie them as symbols on your hands and bind them on your foreheads. Write them on the doorframes of your houses and on your gates. –Deuteronomy 6:5–9

Scripture Affirmations

As you are learning and growing I'd like to leave you with a few affirmations that are rooted in scripture for you to carry in your toolbox when the enemy's voice seems louder than the truth.

Here are some powerful truths to declare over yourself in those times where you forget what you possess.

- I am fearfully and wonderfully made. –Psalm 139:14
- I am chosen. –Jeremiah 1:4
- I have everything I need. –2 Peter 1:3
- I am redeemed. –Colossians 1:13–14
- I am forgiven. –1 John 1:9
- I don't want for nothing. –Psalm 23
- He is my present help. –Psalm 46:1
- I've got the Joy of the Lord. –Nehemiah 8:10
- I have a sound mind. –2 Timothy 1:7

- I am worth more than rubies. –Proverbs 31:10
- God is within me; I will not fall. –Psalm 46:5
- I am not alone. –Deuteronomy 31:8

Encouragement for You

Maybe you're in that place right now doing the best you can, clinging to routines, trying to heal. Don't stop. But also, don't do it without Him. I challenge you to take these truths and insert your name into the scriptures. Speak them over yourself. Write them everywhere. These are more than words—they are reminders that even when you feel stuck, God is still working. His Word never returns void.

You've rehearsed the lies long enough. Now it's time to rehearse the truth. Say it. Believe it. Walk in it. Freedom is already yours.

> You've rehearsed the lies long enough. Now it's time to rehearse the truth. Say it. Believe it. Walk in it. Freedom is already yours.

MY THOUGHTS

✝

CHAPTER FOUR

Just One Touch

Matthew 9:18-26

In Chapter 1, I shared how I was juggling too many responsibilities and how the Lord sat me down. Now, I want to take you deeper into one of those pivotal experiences that followed shortly after.

Like the woman with the issue of blood—who believed that if she could just touch the hem of Jesus' garment, she would be healed—I found myself in desperate need of just a touch myself.

A Desperate Need

In 2020, I purchased a ticket to attend the Women Evolve Conference hosted by Pastor Sarah Jakes Roberts. But due to COVID-19, the conference was canceled and held virtually instead. Later, I received notice that the event would return as an in-person gathering in November 2021. Initially, I decided not to go.

But like I mentioned in Chapter 1—your girl had reached a breaking point. I was drowning. On the brink of homelessness. And just a week before the conference, I felt an urgency in my spirit.

I had to be there.

My name was in the room, and Jesus was there—I mean, you do the math. The only thing holding me back was: How am I going to get there?

A Spark of Faith

As I wrestled with the how, my aunt who lives in Texas came to mind. It felt like a bright idea—but even with that thought, I started listing all the reasons why I couldn't go.

Still, I kept pondering. I began to reflect on the times when I'd been down to nothing—and God came through.

Chicago. Reston, Virginia. San Diego.

Conference after conference, adventure after adventure—He always made a way. None of those events were spiritual, yet He met me there.

So surely… surely, He would come through—especially with His name being attached to the Women Evolve conference.

When you're a child of destiny, there's no such thing as impossible.

Since my aunt lived in Texas, I thought maybe I could stay with her during the conference. But much to my dismay, she lived in San Antonio—and Dallas and San Antonio are eight hours apart.

> When you're a child of destiny, there's no such thing as impossible.

When I shared my plan, she told me, "You have to accept that you've invested in something that won't yield any fruit."

I knew she meant well. In her mind, she was being realistic and concerned about me and my son. From her perspective, it didn't seem practical or wise.

At first, I felt judged. But now I realize—she wasn't judging me; she was genuinely concerned. –1 Corinthians 2:12–16.

I didn't have time to be offended.

I told the Lord plainly, "If You don't want me to go, show me in a way I'll understand."

As I continued my DoorDash deliveries, her words echoed in my mind; "You've invested in something that won't yield any fruit. "That's when it clicked.

The Bible is full of truth about bearing fruit. I mean what's sown in the Spirit always produces something right? And this trip, this step of faith, was an investment into my spiritual growth. –John 15:5

Investing in my spiritual life + Drawing closer to Him = Fruit. That was my confirmation.

With nothing more than a mustard seed of faith, I handed it over to God. When God gives you permission to move, it comes with peace and confirmation—even when the way forward feels impossible.

> When God gives you permission to move, it comes with peace and confirmation— even when the way forward feels impossible.

He is the God of possibility. That conversation lit a fire in me. And that... was all she wrote.

The Process

Stop looking at what you don't have and work with what you do have. I may not have had any money, but guess what? I did have a car. So, I kept earning however I could—mainly through DoorDash. But let me be real: it wasn't enough.

> Stop looking at what you don't have and work with what you do have.

That's when I decided to start driving for Uber.

But before I could even consider it, I had to update my vehicle title and pass an inspection. I was okay with that—especially since I was about to drive all the way to Timbuktu. Just playing.

The inspection cost $125, and the title update was $60. If you remember back in Chapter 1, I had stopped working around this time. I was Door Dashing from dusk till dawn, just trying to earn enough for that inspection. And God made it happen—just like He always does.

Listen, I was getting all kinds of tips. I hit my goal and officially started driving for Uber.

That week—the same week as the conference—I drove nonstop. Mind you, I was starting with almost nothing in my account, and the conference was only four days away. From Monday to Wednesday, I drove from sunup to sundown. I'd drop my son off at school in the morning and hit the road until it was time to pick him up.

By Wednesday night, I dropped him off with my big cousin— the same one who took us in when he was a newborn—so I could make the most of my final push before hitting the road Thursday morning.

Over the course of three days, I earned $600. I thought to myself, Man, I should've been driving for Uber—okayyy!

Little did I know, God was already ordering every step. You'll often hear me say: God is in the details.

We're sitting around waiting on God to make a move, when really He's waiting on you.

The Journey

I hit the road at 8 a.m. on Thursday. My GPS showed I'd arrive by Friday at 6 a.m.—a 22-hour drive. Risky or not, nothing was going to stop me from getting to Him, just like the woman with the issue of blood. I was desperate. I figured that if I could just get close enough, something would change.

> If I could just get close enough, something would change.

Since this was a last-minute decision, I didn't book a hotel. I planned to sleep in my car. In my mind, I figured I could wash up in the bathroom at The Potter's House in Dallas, Texas—because I assumed it would be like a hotel. This was my first "mission" done strictly to encounter Jesus. Other trips had been to see motivational speakers, often in hotel ballrooms—not sanctuaries.

I don't know why I didn't just book a room—especially since I had more funds than usual. I'm grateful that God's thoughts and ways are higher than mine, and His plans are always better than my own.

Ain't Nothing Better Than an Open Road and Jesus

It was scary—unfamiliar roads, pitch-black skies, and nothing but gospel music (and a few R&B jams) to keep me company. Every hour felt like a new test of faith. The roads stretched endlessly ahead, uncertain and unfamiliar. I had no backup plan, no safety net. If something went wrong, I was on my own. Except—I wasn't.

I kept gripping the wheel, crying out, "God, I trust You. I trust You." Every mile was an act of surrender, a declaration that I believed He would see me through. I fought and prayed hard in that car. I must be crazy—who does this? I thought. Fear crept in. Is this why people fly instead of drive to unknown cities?

If there was a negative thought to have, I had it. But I held on because I knew the Lord was with me. I said, "Now Lord, You said You would never leave me nor forsake me. You know I've got to make it back home to Hasaun safely." One of those "I trust You but… listen here now, Sir" kind of prayers. That's how God and I get down.

The only people who knew my whereabouts were my cousin and my son. I called my mom, First Lady, and one of my good sisters from Michigan once I arrived.

He Knows What You Need Before You Do

Around 3 a.m. on Friday, I realized I'd forgotten the basics—**toothpaste, soap, toothbrush—**everything. I still had about five and a half hours left. I figured I'd ask the "hotel receptionist" for these supplies. But I stopped at a gas station/restaurant to use the restroom and decided to look around.

To my surprise, they had everything I needed.

Whattttttt?!?!?!?!?. How many times do we make a plan we think is best, only to find it could've wrecked us—but God steps in and takes care of every detail? –Matthew 6:8 He said all we have to do is trust Him, and He'll handle the rest.

They had everything… except a washcloth.

I asked the cashier if they sold any. She said no. But behind her, I noticed a stack of towels.

"You sell towels, though?" I asked.

"Yes," she replied. "You get one when you buy a shower."

A shower? In a gas station?

"$25," she said. "People come here and shower in the back."

I was shook. "$25 for a shower you install in your house?"

She looked at me sideways. "No... like people take showers here. In the back."

"Ohhh. I see," I said, finally catching on. "Can I get one now?"

She sighed, probably annoyed. "Yes. Unless you're coming back later."

"Nope," I said. "I'll take one now!"

I grabbed my clothes, but as I came back inside, I started to second-guess it. The gas station looked a little run down, and I braced myself for the worst. As soon as I had the thought; The cashier offered to clean the shower before I went in.

And y'all—that shower was luxurious. I was blown away. All I could do was cry and thank Him. He really does care about every detail of our lives. –Luke 12:7

We try so hard to figure everything out. But if we could, why would we need Him? And if we don't need Him, how can He get the glory from our lives?

Arrival at The Potter's House

Refreshed and full of gratitude, I arrived at The Potter's House just in time for registration. Sitting in my car, I worshiped and thanked God for getting me there safely. As I pulled into the parking lot, my hands shook. This was it. I had made it.

Tears filled my eyes. This wasn't just a conference—it was an encounter. I could feel it in my spirit. "God... I'm here." The same God who kept me on the road, who provided for me through strangers, who made a way where there was no way—He was about to do something.

I stepped out of my car and—for the first time in a long time—I could breathe.

Divine Appointments

While in line, I connected with other women. One woman, Ms. Erin, asked where I was staying. When I admitted I'd planned to sleep in my car, she immediately offered to share her hotel room.

Y'all, I gained a bed and a sister in Christ.

Turns out, Ms. Erin was also a minister (I found out on our last night). She prayed with me and prophesied over me. And today? I'm walking in everything the Holy Spirit spoke through her. My time with her was the start of the overflow I'd experience during that three-day conference.

Reflection Prompt

Reflect on a time God placed strangers in your path to bless you. What did He reveal through them?

It Was Divine, Even Down to Our Seats

When it was time to take our seats, an announcement was made anyone with a COVID-19 card could sit closer to the stage. So, you know I took advantage.

I found a seat between two women—Ashley, 33, on my left and Monette, 30, on my right. I was 27 at the time. And y'all… All three of us were:

- Single moms who had our babies when we were teens
- The youngest of four siblings
- Exactly three years apart in age

It was a divine setup. Like the Trinity—Father, Son, and Holy Spirit—we were a God-ordained trio. He wanted to show us we weren't alone. As soon as we realized our connection, Sarah Jakes Roberts started preaching about coming out of the grave.

We stood up, held hands, and shed every dead weight we'd been carrying. It was the most liberating moment of my life.

That was the moment God resurrected me; not physically, but spiritually. I was finally free.

It Was Necessary

The next morning, Ashley sent the song "It Was Necessary" by Fantasia to our group chat. I played the song as I showered.

In the shower, God gave me a vision: I saw myself as a dirty, broken skeleton. He began to wash me clean. I wept. He was cleansing not just my body but my soul.

Right there, I surrendered my life again, fully and completely.

> Sometimes God allows us to be broken–not to punish us, but to remind us that we are His.

This journey was never about what I could handle. It was about learning to trust Him for everything. Sometimes God allows us to be broken—not to punish us, but to remind us that we are His.

The sacrifices of God are a broken spirit; a broken and contrite heart, O God, You will not despise. –Psalm 51:17

> Whether you're in a valley, a dry place, or even on a mountaintop… know this: it is necessary.

The Lord is close to the brokenhearted and saves those who are crushed in spirit. –Psalm 34:18

Whether you're in a valley, a dry place, or even on a mountaintop… know this: it is necessary.

Sometimes, just a touch is all it takes.

My cup was overflowing. My hope—restored. I was on fire. I had come to Texas just needing a touch, but God did more than restore me—He gave me marching orders. I was eager to return home and carry out the assignment the Lord had given me at the conference. There was no confusion, no doubt. I knew exactly what I needed to do next. As soon as my feet hit the ground back home, I was ready to get to work.

MY THOUGHTS

CHAPTER FIVE

Soldier Up

Called to Organize a Women's Conference (AGAIN)!

During my stay in Texas, Pastor Sarah Jake Roberts encouraged the women of God to write down what He had placed in their hearts to pursue. I heard the Lord loud and clear: He told me to organize a women's conference upon my return home.

I was surprised by this instruction, as I had already attempted to organize a women's conference titled "The Time Is Now" earlier in the year. It was a wonderful experience but, one I did entirely on my own—only one person showed up. Nonetheless, it was fruitful. So, when I heard the Lord's prompting to do it again, I knew it was about to go down. I was on fire and I was ready to set the captives free. I just knew it was going to be life-changing for many generations. The ones who went before me and the ones who will be coming after me.

Admitting I Need Help

When I hosted the first conference, The Time Is Now, it makes sense why only one person showed up. One person was all I could handle. Chile, I did not factor in the cost—and I don't just mean the literal one. I definitely didn't have a team. I didn't have the help I needed—because honestly, I didn't have any at the time. I hadn't truly sought His direction on it, yet He still allowed it to be fruitful. Just wait and see how He orchestrated the It's Time to Get Up conference.

I clearly wasn't ready the first time, nor was I doing it under the Lord's leading. We have to be led by the Spirit—especially when we're talking about helping someone heal. Child, being in the "people business" is no joke; you're dealing with folks who've endured years of trauma. You definitely need the Holy Ghost for that. What I was working with before versus what He did later? Yeah, one person was enough then.

The Lord God said, It is not good for man to be alone. –Genesis 2:18

While this verse is often associated with marriage, it also applies to life in general

Two are better than one, because they have a good return for their labor: If either of them falls down, one can help the other up. But pity anyone who falls and has no one to help them up. –Ecclesiastes 4:9–10

I grew up in an era where being independent was seen as a badge of honor. And honestly? I hate that for us.

Challenging the "Independent Woman" Mindset

The world glorifies being an "independent woman" or promotes the idea that "women don't need men." But that's foolishness. Do you remember that jam Webbie came out with—*I-N-D-E-P-E-N-D-E-N-T...*

She got her own house / She got her own car / Two jobs, work hard...

Listen, I was jamming to it back then too! I've still got a little ghetto in me, okay! Don't try me; try Jesus—just kidding, y'all.

I'm not saying you shouldn't be independent, I'm also not saying we should rely too heavily on others. But we weren't created to go it alone. Take Ruth and Naomi, or Mary and Martha, for example—or even look at the women I met at the conference and how we needed one another. We needed each other to push ourselves out of the grave.

There's nothing wrong with depending on others. In fact, we're called to be dependent—on the King of Kings. That's where our hope and trust belong—in Him. Let Him send you the people. Because let me tell you something, people will disappoint you every time—including yourself. But depending on Christ? Now that's our true design. That's our makeup!

Because our Father is limitless, you too are limitless in Him. We have access to His people, His Kingdom, His righteousness, and His resources.

For the earth is the Lord's, and the fullness thereof. –Psalm 24:1

Revelation and Repossession

A few days after returning home from the Women Evolve Conference, I met with one of the women God had placed on my heart to help carry out this plan He instructed. We sat down to discuss the conference we would put together. During our meeting, we were amazed to discover that God had given us the same idea. The women stated He had placed the title "It's Time to Get Up" on her heart, while I had been holding on to "The Time Is Now!"

When God calls you to do something, He confirms it and gives you peace—there's no

> When God calls you to do something, He confirms it and gives you peace–there's no confusion or hesitation.

confusion or hesitation. If you feel doubt or restlessness, chances are it's not from Him, and you should proceed with caution.

We both agreed that "It's Time to Get Up" would be the perfect title for our conference, believing our next step would be to connect with the other people God placed on our hearts to help build His temple aka the conference.

A week after our meeting, my car got repossessed. If it wasn't one thing, it was another. I stepped outside, and my heart immediately dropped. The spot where my car had been empty. Just like that—it was gone. No warning (well, aside from those notices I got months ago, lol). But still, it felt so sudden—no way to stop it. Just gone. I stood there in disbelief. I'd been fighting so hard, pushing through every obstacle, and now this?

I still had a voice, though. So, I picked up the phone. I called the first lady of my church at the time and vented about everything I was going through. She placed me on hold and three-way called another mighty woman of God—one of my wise counselors, my mentor. These two women "pulled me up off the ground" and prayed with and for me for almost two hours. I'd never had that experience before—someone truly interceding on my behalf like that. They started praying for all women and all kinds of things I had never even heard of. That phone call changed my life; it opened my heart to allowing people in.

The Lord will send you the help you need.

Turns out my spiritual father was right: the Lord will send you the help you need. These women became part of my army—like my captains or generals.

They are the epitome of Titus 2 women—beautiful representations of Christ, submitted to Him, committed to Him, and available for

His work. Standing in the gap for families, communities, and the kingdom wasn't something they just talked about; you saw it in how they showed up. They demonstrated what true discipleship is. They walked beside me, prayed me through, and gave me a shoulder to cry on. When my cross was too heavy, they helped me carry it. This is how we ought to be for one another.

The Lord Will Sit You Down

After being refueled by these prayer warriors, I was encouraged to read my Bible. They reminded me I must study to show myself approved—that the Word would sustain me. –2 Timothy 2:15 Honestly, I hadn't opened my Bible much before. I prayed and talked to God, but before He "sat me down," I was one of those people who felt I didn't need church for God to reach me.

Growing up in my household my mom was a Christian, and my dad was a Muslim. From my perspective, we didn't really have anyone to teach us about church or God. Don't get me wrong—my dad made sure we prayed before bedtime and upon waking, but it wasn't a lifestyle so to speak. My grandmother was our only consistent example of Christian faith, but I didn't live with her, so there was no continuity.

I believed I could "have church" or experience the presence of God at home in my living room. While this is true I learned you do need to be in the room with other believers. –Hebrews 10:25 It's a whole different dynamic when it's just you and Jesus versus engaging in corporate worship. My routine was go to church, get a word and do it again the next week. I'd read the Word

Scripture is meant to be for our daily usage.

occasionally, but not every day. I didn't realize Scripture is meant to be for our daily usage. That there was instruction for us daily. I think that's why most of us think "oh another day another dollar" and why we feel so drained and dry because we've been missing our real bread and butter.

> If we're to be like Christ–not to be Him but to be like Him– what better way than to read about Him and learn His ways?

I can see why I needed to be seated. The Lord was taking me back to the basics: meeting with Him and communing with Him. At that time, I no longer had a vehicle. I wasn't working, and I had to put my education on pause. Everything felt like it was in disarray when simultaneously He was bringing me back to my original intent of being. I learned the importance of getting into the Word. So, I studied Jesus and His character. I applied the Scriptures to my life. If we're to be like Christ—not to be Him but to be like Him—what better way than to read about Him and learn His ways?

I mimicked what Jesus did: waking up in the middle of the night, opening the Word, and having conversations with the Father. The more I did this, the less worried I became. The loneliness faded, and I began looking forward to my meetings with Jesus.

Haggai & Zechariah: A Divine Wake-Up Call

One night, while seeking the Father, He led me to the books of Haggai and Zechariah—books I never even knew existed in the bible. The Holy Spirit was checking me, y'all. You'll have to go back and read them for yourself, but here's the message I received from Haggai:

Basically, the Lord was letting me know: Hey, I gave you warning after warning, but you still didn't listen. So now what? You're in a drought, and I caused this drought. You were so caught up in how pretty your walls were but, what about my house; It's in ruins! So here's what you'll do: rebuild my home. And this latter house will be greater than the former. I will get the glory. Don't worry, I'll strengthen and guide you every step of the way.

I was shook. The Lord had deliberately told me He tried to warn me, but I wouldn't listen. I realized my own "house" (my ambition) overshadowed His "house." That explained the many times my car broke down in the middle of the road and why, no matter how hard I worked, nothing went right. Suddenly, those storms and tsunamis I endured made sense. He was right—I'd been more concerned about getting ahead than about what mattered to Him. In my defense, I didn't even know what a real relationship with Him looked like. I just wanted a better position for me and my family.

After reading Haggai, I was filled with awe and humility. Realizing he caused the drought was overwhelming. It also assured me He was serious about me rebuilding His temple (this conference). Not only that—He was trusting me to carry out His will! I dove deeper into Haggai, writing down what I learned and praying fervently. Like a curious child, I asked the Father about every detail, wanting to see how it connected to my life at that moment.

Decision to Get Up

This call was especially impactful because it came during the pandemic, when the world was more hectic than usual. A time when people were losing hope. I faced the inevitable; obey or keep suffering? It felt like stepping up or staying stuck. By God's grace, I was determined to get up.

He has called you by name. Are you going to answer His call? You do realize, it's not only about you; right? Your yes is the breakthrough for someone else. Even more amazing is that He doesn't need us; yet, He chooses us anyhow. What an honor and privilege. He knows we're unqualified, but because He's the One calling, You are already equipped. You are His workmanship, created in Christ Jesus for good works, which God prepared in advance for you to do –Ephesians 2:10.

Reflection

What areas of your life might God be calling you to rebuild
for His glory? How will you respond to His call today?

Take Up Your Cross

To fulfill God's calling on your life, you must give up your own life. This means letting go of control and how you want things to be—releasing your children, spouse, career, family, and everything else into God's hands. If anyone would come after me, let him deny himself, take up his cross, and follow me. For whoever would save his life will lose it, but whoever loses his life for my sake will find it. –Matthew 16:24

> To fulfill God's calling on your life, you must give up your own life.

We must die to our flesh daily. If we don't, we leave no room for the Holy Spirit to work in us. Taking up your cross means aligning your desires with God's will, even if it requires sacrifices and challenges begin to spark up.

You might wonder how to "lose your life" for His sake. I asked the same question when He brought me to this passage. Reflecting on how awesome He is, I realized that when He says our steps are ordered, He means it. He says, "I know the plans I have for you." The Lord first stirred my soul to fight by placing me in a position of no return, then gave me an assignment that He later confirmed through another person. He's so good that He even showed me how to fulfill the assignment: by denying my own wants and learning to desire what He wants for me. Sometimes I found myself surrendering all day long. I would acknowledge my desires to the Lord and ask Him to remove them until I desired Him more. It was that simple.

The Ultimate Sacrifice

In January 2022, the kids were headed back to school after winter break. If you recall, the pandemic was still ongoing, and I wasn't comfortable with my son returning to the building. My nephews— my sister's sons—were still learning from home because their school hadn't reopened yet. I expressed my concerns to my son's school, and thankfully, they were understanding and allowed him to continue learning from home.

Wanting to be obedient to God's command to take up my cross, I made the bold decision to send my son to stay with my sister for a month. During that time, I allowed no contact between us.

This was one of the hardest sacrifices I've ever made. Sure, I was used to dropping him off for a day or two for my mini-adventures, but a whole month felt like forever. He had never been away that long. I had to trust that God had his back and release my own fears.

That first night, I sat in my son's room. Honestly, every time he's away, I sleep in his bed. As I laid there, the silence settled into my chest. It was too quiet. I knew this was what God was asking me to do, but everything in me wanted to undo it—call my sister, pick him up, bring him home. Had I made a mistake? What if he needed me? These thoughts raced through my mind. All I could say was, "Lord, I trust You."

My thought was, if I released my responsibilities for that time, it would give me space for uninterrupted one-on-one time with Jesus, so we could generate a plan together. I was taking Him at His word. Child, I cried the entire month—no lie. While the sacrifice broke me, it also caused me to tap into a strength I didn't know I had. I was so lost and didn't understand anything I was doing. I kept playing "Victory" by Brenda Waters and singing it aloud just to make it through.

Sending my son away forced me to confront my fears and surrender fully to God. It was a pivotal moment that taught me how to trust Him completely.

I meditated a lot on how the Father created the heavens and the earth in seven days, and I focused on how He had plans for me –Jeremiah 29:11: My plan was to seek His will and come up with a strategy—but instead, I mostly cried.

By the time my son returned home, I still didn't have a clear plan.

Yet while I didn't leave that month with a blueprint, I walked away with something more valuable: a better understanding of how to seek Him. There's a song that says, "Praise will confuse the enemy." So I shouted my way through. I declared that no weapon formed against me would prosper –Isaiah 54:17 and spoke His Word back to Him. I waged war in the spirit. I got on my knees, I surrendered, and I stood on the promise that He'd never leave me. I even woke up in the middle of the night like Jesus did—spending time with the Father.

Most of the time, I didn't even know how to approach Him. But I simply said, "Here I am, Lord, trusting You." And in His faithfulness, He revealed Himself in ways that assured me He was listening. Even when it felt like He wasn't doing anything, I kept pressing forward.

He hears you, too.

Take up your cross. His plan is far greater than the one you have for yourself.

He is your Creator. And the calling on your life will cost you something—but it's worth it.

Reflection and Action

What are you willing to sacrifice or lose in order to follow Jesus?

Write down that thing you just cant live without. Then choose to give it up today to focus on Him. Maybe it's a relationship. Maybe it's control. Maybe it's fear.

Whatever it is—write it down. Hold it in your hands. Then, as an act of faith, rip it up, burn it, or lay it at the altar.

And when you do, declare out loud: " Lord, I surrender my past… I give you… It is yours. Help me to not pick it back up In Jesus Name Amen"

Watch how He moves in your life when you finally let go.

Keep what you've written in sight. Let it be a reminder that surrender, and sacrifice are ongoing processes. Knowing this, it may look different in every season.

We soldier up by admitting we need help and keeping our hearts open to receive it.

> We soldier up by admitting we need help and keeping our hearts open to receive it.

MY THOUGHTS

CHAPTER SIX

He's Preparing Me

Finally, be strong in the Lord and in His mighty power. Put on the full armor of God, so that you can take your stand against the devil's schemes. –Ephesians 6:10–12

During this season, there was a song I played almost every day. Lady Janelle introduced me to it: He's Preparing Me by Daryl Coley. There's a line that lit me on fire every single time: "The Lord didn't call no coward soldiers."

> "The Lord didn't call no coward soldiers."

That's all I needed to hear and I'd be on go mode! Girl I put on my entire armor of God faithfully. Because a coward I am not. I may get weak, may need to cry, huff and puff whatever but we fighters and giving up is not an option. We were built for this.

So, what does the full armor of God really consist of?

- The belt of truth
- The breastplate of righteousness
- The gospel of peace on your feet
- The shield of faith

- The helmet of salvation
- The sword of the Spirit
- And prayer

> The moment you wake up, the enemy is already seeking to devour you. This is why your armor must stay on—day and night, even while you sleep.

The moment you wake up, the enemy is already seeking to devour you. This is why your armor must stay on—day and night, even while you sleep. For our struggle is not against flesh and blood, but against the rulers, against the authorities, against the powers of this dark world, and against the spiritual forces of evil in the heavenly realms –Ephesians 6:12.

We are constantly at war—often without even realizing it. That's why the smallest things irritates you: the driver who cuts you off, the kids not listening, even the toilet seat left up. Before you know it, you're apologizing to the Lord for snapping or acting out of character.

And why does that happen?

Because you're out here naked.

Life happens—and it's going to happen. In this world, you will have trouble –John 16:33. But thank God for Jesus and the armor He's given to every one of His sons and daughters. That's how we navigate this world without being consumed by it—by putting on the full armor of God. We are in this world, but not of it –John 15:19.

So let's break down each piece of armor—and how to use it.

Reflective Question

As you read, consider: Where have I been leaving myself exposed, and how can I put on God's armor today?

The Belt of Truth

What do you use a belt for? To keep your pants from falling, to tighten your waist, or to pull your outfit together. Basically, a belt holds everything in place.

The belt of truth works the same way—God's truth holds us together when life tries to pull us apart.

It's vital to know the difference between truth and lies. The Bible warns us: Beware of false prophets, who come to you in sheep's clothing but inwardly are ravenous wolves –Matthew 7:15. Not everyone who says to me, "Lord, Lord," will enter the kingdom of heaven, but only those who do the will of my Father –Matthew 7:21–23. To discern truth from lies, we must study God's Word and show ourselves approved –2 Timothy 2:15.

His Word keeps us grounded, steady, and whole—even when everything around us is falling apart. He is the Great I AM. He is the Way, the Truth, and the Life –John 14:6. Without His truth, we will crash and burn. Period.

Real-Life Moment

When God gives you a promise or vision, but it doesn't come right away, you often end up in the in-between. That's where I was while trying to finish this book. I knew what God said. I knew the promise. But there were nights I literally cried and yelled in frustration because I didn't think I was going to make it to the finish line.

I had to keep it real with the Lord:

"Listen, I need Your help. I feel so insecure. This is the only thing You've given me, and I don't think I can finish it."

I was honest about what I had been feeling but never expressed aloud. I was listening to those nagging lies again:

- "You're not going to make it."
- "You're stuck."
- "You will not cross the finish line."

Even though I knew the Word and could speak it, I wasn't standing on it—until I broke down and admitted my need for help. Sometimes it takes a breakdown for a breakthrough.

Once I did admit my need for help that's when things shifted. That's when I stood on the truth:

When I am weak, then I am strong –2 Corinthians 12:10.

I can do all things through Christ who strengthens me –Philippians 4:13.

So now I ask you:

- What's holding you together these days?
- What are you standing on—truth or lies?

Your belt of truth secures your foundation. But life doesn't just test what you know—it targets what you feel and who knows? That our feelings will get us in trouble every single time. We cannot allow our feelings and emotions to be the driving force of our lives. That's why the breastplate is next.

The Breastplate of Righteousness

A breastplate covers the heart, chest, and vital organs—your most vulnerable, life-sustaining parts. Without it, you're an easy target.

In the same way, righteousness protects your heart—your character, your motives, your posture before God. –Ephesians 6:14 reminds us to Stand firm then, with the belt of truth buckled around your waist, with the breastplate of righteousness in place. Notice how Paul links truth and righteousness together—its what hold us up and protects us.

But this isn't our righteousness—it's El Tsidkenu, the Lord Our Righteousness, covering us through Christ. Righteousness isn't just about right actions—it's about being in right standing before God, made possible by grace.

Scriptures to Remember

- This righteousness is given through faith in Jesus Christ to all who believe. –Romans 3:22
- God made Him who had no sin to be sin for us, so that in Him we might become the righteousness of God. –2 Corinthians 5:21
- All our righteous acts are like filthy rags. –Isaiah 64:6
- The Lord is righteous in all His ways and faithful in all He does. –Psalm 145:17

The breastplate guards you from pride, bitterness, and self-righteousness—especially when you've been hurt or misunderstood. It's a daily reminder to stay humble, alert, and pure. Guard your heart above all else, for it determines the course of your life –Proverbs 4:23.

Real-Life Moment

My son had a school project due a few days after it was assigned. I noticed he wasn't working on it, so I asked if he needed help. Confidently, he said no. The day it was due, the teacher extended the deadline by a week.

This time, I had him present the project to me. I suggested a few improvements, but you can imagine the attitude: "Ughhh, my teacher said it was fine!"

Each time the deadline came, the teacher extended it again. I kept nudging him, but no progress. Finally, frustrated, I prayed: "Now Daddy (Jesus), I know You see this. I've been gracious. I haven't yelled, haven't snapped—but the moment I do, I'm wrong!"

That's when the Holy Spirit told me to step back. And what I saw in my son… was myself. The way I delay obedience. The way I drag my feet until the last minute. Suddenly, I saw God's grace through the teacher—extending deadlines, covering him while he was still learning. Just like He had been doing with me.

His grace is sufficient in our weakness. His righteousness covers us when we're delayed, hesitant, or imperfect. That moment blew me away.

You see, both my son and I were growing in that season. That's why we must put on the breastplate—because we don't always know someone else's process. And honestly, don't we all receive undeserved grace every single day?

Create in me a clean heart, O God, and renew a right spirit within me. –Psalm 51:10

Feet Shod with the Preparation of the Gospel of Peace

What does it mean to have your feet shod with the Gospel of Peace? It means that when God sends you into different atmospheres, you don't show up "bumping knuck if you buck right." You show up with maturity and poise—not because you have it all together, but because the One who holds you together is the One who sent you. El Shalom— the God of Peace—walks with you.

Being shod with the Gospel of Peace also means you are ready. Ready to go wherever God sends, carrying His message of hope, His presence, and His peace. Your feet aren't just stable—they are equipped for action, prepared to bring calm, encouragement, and truth to every place and person He leads you to.

When you step into rooms where you were once wounded, you don't drag the past with you—you carry healing and peace. You've spent time with the Word. You've studied to show yourself approved. –2 Timothy 2:15 So now, when others are unraveling, you don't come undone—you come equipped.

When someone breaks down in tears, you don't panic. You carry peace—governed not by emotion, but by His Spirit. This is why it's so important to let the Lord direct your steps. He doesn't send us anywhere randomly—He anoints us for specific places and people. We weren't created to wander. We were designed to be planted—like trees by rivers of living water. And your leaves? They will not wither –Psalm 1:3. Peace is one of the fruits of the Spirit –Galatians 5:22–23. When your feet are covered in the preparation of the Gospel of Peace, you don't just talk about peace—you walk it out.

Blessed are the peacemakers, for they will be called children of God. –Matthew 5:9

And the peace of God, which surpasses all understanding, will guard your hearts and your minds in Christ Jesus. –Philippians 4:7

Jesus demonstrated this peace during a storm.

In Matthew 8:23–27, the disciples panicked, but Jesus? Calm. Unbothered. Even in chaos, He trusted God completely. When they woke Him in fear, He said, "Peace, be still," and the storm obeyed.

That's the peace we carry—a peace that equips us, steadies us, and readies us to move. Walking in peace prepares you for every challenge, and faith is the hand you raise when life comes at you fast.

The Shield of Faith

In this walk as a believer, there's one thing you cannot live without—and that is faith.

The Word puts it this way:

Without faith, it is impossible to please God. –Hebrews 11:6

The just shall live by faith. –Hebrews 10:38

Now faith is confidence in what we hope for and assurance about what we do not see. –Hebrews 11:1

One thing my spiritual father often would point out to me was: I was "good when I can see the signs—but when God goes silent, when He stops sending people my way, that's when doubt creeps in."

Whew. Your girl fails that test every time. I've gotten better, but let's just say I've had plenty of practice. These days, I'd say I have crazy faith. Straight up though—even with crazy faith—it can still be hard to hold on when reality doesn't match what you're believing for. What we stand on often goes against what we see. That's the real fight—the battle between what you feel and what you know, what you see versus what is true.

But that's exactly when you must pick up the **shield of faith** and declare, even in the silence:

- "I will make it to the other side."
- "My child will come home."
- "I will be healed."

Why? Because He has already spoken. His Word is enough. He is not a man that He should lie. –Numbers 23:19 And His Word never returns void. –Isaiah 55:11

Lady Janelle would always remind me:

"Don't dig in doubt what you planted in faith and declared on the mountain top."

Even with tears in your eyes, when all you have is Jesus, believe that He is enough. He does the impossible. I quit my job to follow Him, and He carried me—and continues to carry me. It's been mind-blowing.

We are called to live completely dependent on Him. A life with Christ is a life of faith.

What Is the Shield of Faith?

The shield of faith is our defense against doubt, fear, and spiritual attacks.

Above all, take up the shield of faith, with which you can extinguish all the flaming arrows of the evil one. –Ephesians 6:16

So, what does that look like in real life?

- When the enemy whispers, "God won't come through for you", lift your shield and declare: My God shall supply all my needs. –Philippians 4:19
- When fear says, "This is too much," lift your shield and say: God has not given me a spirit of fear, but of power, love, and a sound mind. –2 Timothy 1:7
- When disappointment tempts you to walk away, lift your shield and pray: Lord, I believe. Help my unbelief. –Mark 9:24

Faith isn't a feeling. It's a knowing. It's a response rooted not only in God's Word but in your experiences with Him.

> Faith isn't a feeling. It's a knowing.

Just like a physical shield must be lifted to protect, your faith must be activated—spoken aloud, stood upon, and walked out. Faith without works is dead. –James 2:17

Why It Matters

Life will come swinging. Without faith, you'll believe the lies, shrink instead of stand, retreat instead of run your race.

But when your shield is up, nothing can stand against you.

If you have faith as small as a mustard seed, you can say to this mountain, 'Move from here to there,' and it will move. Nothing will be impossible for you. –Matthew 17:20

And if the Lord doesn't move that mountain immediately, ask Him for strength to climb it, to push it, and to persevere with His power. You must pick up your shield, lift your head, and walk in faith.

Reflective Question

*Where is my faith being tested today, and
how can I lift my shield right now?*

The Helmet of Salvation

When you think of a helmet, you think of protection—whether on a motorcycle, a bike, or playing a sport. Likewise, when we put on the helmet of salvation, we are protecting our minds. If the enemy can throw you off your rails and make you doubt or forget what God has spoken, that's all he needs. And I'm not just talking about promises of healing, elevation, or provision—this is about the greater promise of your identity in Christ.

As daughters of a King, walking out our salvation, we grow through seasons of waiting—for instruction, for God to move, for promises to unfold. In those moments, your mind will be tested. You'll feel frustration. You'll endure long-suffering where your character is stretched. You'll face lies, accusations, sickness, heartbreak—the whole nine. But here's the truth: if we don't have our helmet on, we're in big trouble.

My mom used to say when I wasn't following instructions:

"If you had a brain, you'd be dangerous."

And honestly? If we truly used the mind of Christ that's been given to us, we would be dangerous to the enemy.

Let this mind be in you, which was also in Christ Jesus –Philippians 2:5

The mind alone is a battlefield. Without the helmet of salvation, we end up living out of emotions and feelings instead of truth. Let's be real, women—we are naturally emotional beings. That's our nature. But salvation gives us access to a new nature. That's why we must constantly bring our thoughts and feelings under the authority of God's Word. It's not about how we feel—it's about what our Father says.

The helmet isn't something you fight for— it's something you already have in Christ. Salvation is your secure position. You fight from victory, not for it.

You fight from victory, not for it.

Scriptures to remember

- You will keep in perfect peace those whose minds are steadfast, because they trust in You. –Isaiah 26:3
- Do not conform to the pattern of this world but be transformed by the renewing of your mind. –Romans 12:2
- We take captive every thought to make it obedient to Christ. –2 Corinthians 10:5
- Let us be sober, putting on faith and love as a breastplate, and the hope of salvation as a helmet. –1 Thessalonians 5:8

This is a spiritual battle, sis. We don't fight like the world does, period. Guard your mind daily. Renew it with truth. Stand firm knowing salvation already covers you. Because when your mind is secure, the enemy loses his grip.

Your mind is covered, your thoughts protected—but what happens when life tries to push back? That's when the sword of the Spirit comes in. God's Word gives you the words and the power to speak truth into every fight.

Reflective Question

*How am I protecting my mind today, and am I
standing fully in the assurance of my salvation?*

Sword of the Spirit

When I blow the trumpet, I and all that are with me, then blow ye the trumpets also on every side of all the camp, and say, The sword of the Lord, and of Gideon. –Judges 7:20

God called Gideon to rise up and set the captives free, but he had to move in alignment with God's instructions. At first, Gideon didn't believe he had what it took—until he began to declare what the Lord declared. When he stepped out of the way, the Spirit had no choice but to rise.

And here's the fun part—you get to personalize this! Just like Gideon, when you step into your battles, declare the Word of God as your weapon. Say it aloud: "The Sword of the Lord and [Your Name]." Go ahead—insert your name. Own it. The Word is alive, and you are its carrier.

As daughters of the King, it's imperative that our thinking lines up with God's thinking. The sword we're talking about isn't physical. We're not cutting steaks—it's the Word of God. You and I must come to a place where we are literally speaking the Word. For the Word of God is alive and active. Sharper than any double-edged sword, it penetrates even to dividing soul and spirit, joints and marrow; it judges the thoughts and attitudes of the heart. –Hebrews 4:12

> You and I must come to a place where we are literally speaking the Word.

Your words have power. Life and death are in the power of the tongue, and those who love it will eat its fruit. –Proverbs 18:21 That's why our words must align with God's Word. My spiritual father used to say, "Don't let people make a joke about you proclaiming you are something you aren't—stand on business and declare, 'I am not that.'"

> Your words have power.

When war rises against you—and it will—you have the authority to speak a thing and see it come to pass. All you have to do is wield the Sword of the Spirit—the Word. When we fail to use our sword and instead operate out of feelings and emotions, we give the enemy ground and misrepresent our Father. For we are Christ's ambassadors. –2 Corinthians 5:20

A Personal Story

When I was younger, I had a smart mouth. Most of the fights I got into were because of it. Don't get it twisted I handled business when I needed to. I ain't always been saved. Lol. But thank the Lord, He saves!

One morning, I was praying in the Spirit really heavy for a particular person and their family. The prayers that went up were intense. Right before church service, I received a text that immediately triggered me. Normally, I would've clapped back in my flesh. But this time, I recognized it—this wasn't about the person. This was the enemy.

During worship, I fought—with the Sword of the Spirit. I declared the truth. I prayed. I swung that sword in the Spirit and I knew hell was mad at me that day because I was on fire. Later, when I got home, my flesh was still pierced, my pride was still boiling. I vented to the Lord about how angry I was. Yet once I cooled down, I had to admit: Wow... this is what it means to fight in the Spirit.

The Lord will fight for you; you need only to be still –Exodus 14:14.

I didn't have to defend myself. I didn't have to confront or "handle" it. I just needed to stand still and tell that devil to go. The very thing that used to get me in trouble—my mouth—is now the very thing God uses as a weapon. Aligned with the Sword of the Lord, it carries the power to set a generation free.

Reflective Question

*Where in your life do you need to stop swinging in the flesh
and pick up your Sword of the Spirit? How will you declare
the Word—personally and boldly—into that situation?*

Prayer: The Final Piece of Armor

Pray in the Spirit on all occasions with all kinds of prayers and
requests. –Ephesians 6:18

Prayer is often the piece of armor we overlook, but it's the power
that keeps everything else working. Your tears are prayers. Your sighs
are prayers. And when you don't know what to say, the Spirit steps in
to intercede for you:

We do not know what we ought to pray for, but the Spirit Himself
intercedes for us through wordless groans. –Romans 8:26

Prayer is simply a conversation with God. It's sharing your wins,
your struggles, your frustrations, everything. The more we commune
with Him, the more equipped we become. Prayer doesn't just move
mountains—it changes you, reshapes your heart, and aligns your
mind with His.

A Real-Life Moment

One morning, I picked my son up from my cousin's house. Traffic
was nuts. I asked him if he'd said his morning prayers. He said he
forgot. So I told him I'd lead us in prayer, and he could close it out.
When it was his turn, he went silent. I nudged him a little, because
it wasn't like he'd never prayed before. Finally, he yelled, "I DON'T
KNOW WHAT YOU WANT ME TO SAY… It's easier to talk to you
and other people than to talk to God!"

At that moment, the Holy Spirit dropped a revelation in my heart. I said, "Son, you talk to your dad, and you can't see him—but you still talk to him. Baby, that's how it is with God too. You may not see Him, but He's listening—and He responds. Always."

Later, I reflected. First off, that revelation was bananas. I cannot wait to see how my son comes to truly know God, because that connection is already so powerful. Just imagine when the Lord truly reveals Himself to Hasaun—glory hallelujah in advance!

It made me think about how personal God's revelation really is. Has He ever revealed Himself to you? Do you remember that moment—the way it felt when you knew it was Him? If you haven't had that experience, I'm telling you—it's one you'll never forget.

I also thought about what Hasaun said. I mean, he was right. Sometimes talking to people is easier. You get answers, reassurance, and immediate feedback. Sometimes, you just need some flesh to vent to.

While that's true, we can't let our need for instant gratification replace our need to talk to God. Carry each other's burdens, and in this way you will fulfill the law of Christ. –Galatians 6:2 Yes, God allows us to lean on people, but if we are wise we would lean on Him first.

Why It Matters

> Prayer isn't just for your benefit— it's for those around you.

Prayer isn't just for your benefit—it's for those around you. You can lift others up, intercede for friends, family, even your community. I wouldn't be where I am today without people praying over me. If praying out loud feels awkward, write your prayers instead. That's actually how I began. Prayer is a gift—and like any weapon, it must be used wisely.

That's the final piece of armor—the one that holds all the others together. Your belt of truth, breastplate of righteousness, and shield of faith work best when prayer flows through them. Your mind, heart, and feet stay covered. Your sword stays sharp. Prayer is what activates your full armor.

So wherever you are today, start the conversation. Prayer keeps you positioned and connected to Heaven's power so that when the battles come, you're not fighting from your flesh but by the Spirit. Let's be real, sis—every day we're in a fight, just not the kind the world sees.

The Battle Is Spiritual

Being a follower of Christ means we no longer fight the way the world does. We use our praise as our weapon.

The saying, "Sticks and stones may break my bones, but words will never hurt," doesn't apply to believers in Christ. Words do hurt—but His Word cuts through every lie, every tactic, every scheme, and every plot set against us—including the lies we tell ourselves.

One of the biggest mistakes we make is enduring our problems through a human lens. We see our sickness as just medical, our depression as just emotional, and our brokenness as just personal. But the truth? It's all spiritual and intentional. That's why it's so important to see things through the lens of Christ. One of the most powerful weapons we have in this fight is worship.

> One of the biggest mistakes we make is enduring our problems through a human lens.

When we don't see things through Christ's lens, our minds begin to spiral—and that's when we fall prey to the enemy's foolishness. Satan doesn't expect you to give God glory after a cancer diagnosis, or praise His holy name when you're told you may never walk again, or after a loved one passes away. If he can get into your mind and make you believe it's over, that's all he needs.

See, he already knows you will overcome—that you already have the victory in all things. You just have to know it for yourself.

When you allow the joy of the Lord to be your strength and decide, "I'm going to praise Him anyhow," that's when breakthroughs happen and healing takes place. Your faith kicks in because you can look back at what God has already done—how He kept food in your fridge, clothes on your back, and sustained you in the moments only you and He know about.

Praise removes worry, brings peace, and brings clarity.

Just say right now:

"Lord, I trust You. I may not be where I want to be, but thank You, I'm not where I used to be." Amen!

Here's the thing about praise—it's not for God; it's for you.

Ways to Actively Fight Spiritual Battles as You Walk in Purpose

Do not let me being a woman of God fool you—I've had plenty of days where I wanted to give up and throw in the towel. Instead of running, I fought back. Day by day, my faith grew stronger, and little by little, I began to witness God move on my behalf.

Here are some ways I learned to fight back:

- **Daily Prayer**

- **Reading & Studying the Word**
- **Worship**
- **Accountability Partners**
- **Fasting & Praying**
- **Journaling**
- **Devotionals**
- **Christian Books / Self-Help**
- **Physical Activity**

Even with all these tools, life gets heavy. And instead of fighting, we freeze. We allow our dreams and goals to gather dust because we give in to fear, doubt, and worry. We let the voices around us drown out the voice of God—too busy focusing on what's happening to us rather than what's happening for us.

I don't care how long it's been, sis—**His promise still stands:**

He who began a good work in you will carry it on to completion. –Philippians 1:6

If He said it, He will do it—period! You just gotta do your part.

I know that's not always easy. Life can disappoint, and things don't always work out the way we hoped. But some doors had to close so you could walk through the right ones. You'll never enter the doors meant for you if you keep looking at the shoulda, coulda, woulda.

> You'll never enter the doors meant for you if you keep looking at the shoulda, coulda, woulda.

One way to keep moving forward is by studying the lives of the brothers and sisters who went before us—not only in the Word, but also by connecting with the leaders in your life. Open your eyes, sis, and really see what's around you and what you have access to that would pull you forward.

Who are you connected to?

When I think of Joseph, I see perseverance. He didn't allow abandonment or betrayal to stop him from continuing to fight—even in unfamiliar territory, surrounded by people he didn't know. He chose to bloom where he was planted. His story reminds us that even in uncomfortable places, God's plan is still unfolding.

Then there's Esther—who stood strong and bold for her bloodline and those connected to her. She was a queen, but even then, you couldn't go before the king unless summoned. When Esther learned the enemy was after her people, she may have hesitated, but she stood. Even with fear and trembling, she said, And if I perish, I perish. –Esther 4:16.

In other words: "Lord, I'm not sure about this, but I will go. I may die or lose some blood on the way, but I am available to You."

She fought differently—through fasting and prayer. And the beautiful part? She had riders who fasted and prayed with her.

Let me ask you something, sis:

Do you have riders in your corner—people who will fast and pray with you, who will tear down a nation and build one up? I'm talking about folk who will go to war with you—hands and knees, crying out for your child to get up out of the streets. Warring beside you as you believe for a baby after being told you can't conceive. Sisters who will just sit with you in silence after receiving devastating news. –Isaiah 58:1–14

When I talk about fasting, I'm not talking about losing weight like the world does. Nawl, sis—fasting means emptying yourself of yourself. I'm not talking about starving yourself either. No—it's dying to your own will and allowing the Holy Spirit to take His rightful place.

Prayer and fasting go hand in hand:

This kind only comes out by fasting and praying. –Matthew 17:21

This strategy ain't nothing new. Many men and women before us prayed and fasted to grow through what they faced in their time—Moses, Daniel, Anna, Hannah, and even Jesus, just to name a few. Their faith gives us a roadmap to persevere today.

What an honor to have those examples—He is the same God yesterday, today, and forevermore. The Bible truly is our Basic Instruction Before Leaving Earth.

However, instructions only work when we follow them. The Word doesn't just prepare us for Heaven (and I know that's where we're trying to get to)—it equips us for the battles we face right here on Earth. We can experience Heaven on Earth now. You do know that, right? The Bible says, "Let Your will be done on earth as it is in Heaven."

Every story, every promise, every command reminds us that we were never meant to fight alone. The same God who gave the instruction also fights on our behalf. Whatever you bind on earth will be bound in Heaven, and whatever you loose on earth will be loosed in Heaven –Matthew 18:18.

The Battle Belongs to God

When we take our positions in faith, when we stand firm in obedience, when we choose to praise and trust Him in the middle of the storm—that's when Heaven moves. He fights on our behalf. He sees what we cannot see, moves in ways we cannot predict, and His promises never fail.

Do not be afraid or discouraged because of this vast army. The battle is not yours, but God's. Take up your positions; stand firm and see the deliverance the Lord will give you… the Lord will be with you. –2 Chronicles 20:15

Sis, the battle was never yours to begin with. It's always belonged to God. –Exodus 14:14

Your Only Job Is to Show Up

Show up and stand your ground.

Worship when it hurts.

Trust when it doesn't make sense.

When you do, He steps in. He sends confusion to the enemy's camp and turns what was meant for harm into the very thing that propels you forward.

Once the dust settles and the shouting stops, that's when the real test begins. When you allow God to move, the enemy can't stand against you.

But baby, the moment we think we're in the clear, here come the distractions. Satan's sly self will do everything in his power to steal your focus, and sis, we fall for it every time –John 10:10.

We've got to recognize his schemes and stop being so gullible. That's why staying alert and guarding your focus is just as important as putting on the armor.

Let's talk about what that looks like.

Getting Rid of Those Distractions

Distractions are everywhere, and let's face it—staying focused is hard. I struggle with being still all the time; I get bored quickly, and if something grabs my attention, it's a wrap. Because really, why would someone put that butterfly right there and expect me not to stop and stare? Or leave a fabulous, shiny something out and expect me not to get caught up in a 30-minute conversation when I should've been cleaning the porch? Those are minor examples, but hopefully, you're tracking with me. Growth, progress, and purpose demand discipline and intention.

Instead of letting the chaos of life dictate your day, try pausing and redirecting your focus. Just because something doesn't go as planned doesn't mean you give up on the rest of the day. Every moment—even the frustrating or seemingly wasted ones—shouldn't stop your hustle and flow. Here are some practical ways I've learned to stay focused, disciplined, and productive, starting with shifting your perspective:

1. Shift Your Perspective

Ask, "What is God teaching me right now?" Or, "Lord, give me eyes to see things the way You do." Even simple questions like these can shift your mindset and move you from frustration to purpose. It doesn't have to be complicated—just ask. As my momma would say, "A closed mouth don't get fed."

2. Recognize Your Limits

I never wanted anyone else to endure what I went through. So, I made myself constantly available to help others. I'm sure you can relate. My heart was in the right place, but eventually, I burned out. I had to face a hard truth: sometimes our good intentions can interfere with what God is trying to do in someone else's life—as well as in our own.

You can't help everybody—and that's okay. Do what you can, but most importantly, know yourself. Know what you can and can't handle. Even Jesus took time to rest and withdraw to pray. Rest isn't selfish—it's stewardship. When you care for yourself, you make room for God to strengthen and refill you for what's next.

3. Learn to Say "No"

Say this aloud: "No is a healthy word."

Adopt the mindset that you just can't help everyone. No is healthy. No is healthy. No is healthy.

Besides, folks have no problem telling you no. You aren't God—He will help whoever it is you're feeling bad about not helping.

Ask yourself, "Where do I need to start saying no so I can say yes to God?"

Getting rid of distractions isn't just about being more productive—it's about being more present with God. When you clear the clutter, you create space for Him to move, speak, and lead.

Making Room for God's Work

Every time I tried to do what God asked—or just stay productive—I found myself caught in the same cycle of distractions. I'd constantly watch TV or oversleep, letting these habits rob me of the chance to seize the day. It was easier to zone out in front of the screen than to put in the work required to reach my goals.

I would say, "Just one more episode," but that one episode turned into an entire day of binge-watching. By the time the next day rolled around, I'd repeat the mistake, feeling guilty and disappointed.

Proverbs 6:9–11: "You lazy people, how long are you going to lie there? When will you get up? You say, 'I need a rest. I think I'll take a short nap.' But then you sleep and sleep and become poorer and poorer."

For me, distractions came in all kinds of forms—not just sleep or too much TV, but also endless scrolling on social media. I'd tell myself I was "just checking" something, and before I knew it, an hour had passed. It wasn't sinful, but it was robbing me of time I could have spent with God—or working on something far more meaningful. After nearly a year of this cycle, I decided enough was enough.

I realized I needed to step out of my comfort zone. Doing all my work at home, where I tended to relax, made it too easy to slip back into old habits. Instead, I started switching up my routine: I'd go to the library, study outside on nice days, or work at a coffee shop. These places really helped because they provided a change of scenery. I saw other people on the move or working, and the lighting was better—it was just a vibe. Changing my environment forced me to stay focused and broke the cycle of procrastination—learn to switch it up.

Reflection

What is distracting you, or what are
you allowing to distract you?

Once I started cutting distractions, God had room to move in my life. Let me show you what that looked like. This all happened during the same season when my mindset began to shift—the same season I attended the Lisa Nichols Abundance Now event.

Personal Story – A Turning Point

I used to smoke cigarettes—packs a day. I was so addicted that I had no shame asking people for a cigarette if I didn't have any, or even bumming 50 cents to buy singles. It got so bad that if I found one on the ground, I'd pick it up and light it.

But God has a way of letting you know when it's time to give something up. He does it in ways that never cease to amaze. One day, I was walking with my son and noticed a woman pushing a cart full of belongings. I admired her pretty pink attire and complimented her on it. She smiled and thanked me, then looked me straight in the eye and said, "You're too pretty to smoke those. You know those could kill you!"

I replied, "I know. I want to stop, and I will soon." She smiled again and continued on her way. I turned my head for just a second, and when I looked back, she was gone. To this day, I believe she was an angel; there's no way she vanished that quickly without a trace.

A few weeks later, I was walking with my son again to the store when I saw two boys—one about 14, the other around 8. The older boy was smoking a cigarette and handed it to the younger one. Watching that scene made me sick to my stomach. All I could see was my own 5-year-old son following in my footsteps—and I was not going to let that happen. I knew I had to get rid of this habit, and I had to do it fast.

That wake-up call forced me to take a hard look at what else in my life needed to change. For months, I'd been craving a healthier lifestyle—mind, body, and spirit. I decided to start waking up in the middle of the night. I'd put my workout gear on and walk up a hill near my house. As I walked, I listened to gospel music and let the pavement carry me, one step at a time. Initially, it was hard—I was constantly out of breath—but I was determined to quit. The more I showed up, the more it felt like a reward. I began to enjoy the dark, lonely night; it gave me a sense of freedom and peace.

At the time, I was in a relationship with J, and our relationship was showing signs of strain. We were living together, and J was also a smoker. He had a nasty cough that irritated me to no end. I became determined to become healthier and rid myself of this filthy habit.

Meanwhile, he would still be asleep. I'd get mad and tell him he needed to get up and join me. "We need to do this together!" I'd insist. Eventually, he started walking with me during those late-night hours, but as I desired a different kind of life, it became clear we were heading in opposite directions. I grew mean and irritable about everything he did. I was so turned off I didn't even want to kiss him, let alone be intimate.

We weren't just growing apart; we were building on sand. And God is a jealous God. That relationship wasn't aligned with Him, and it wasn't built to last.

I knew I was done with smoking for good one particular night. As usual, I woke up in the middle of the night, put on my workout gear, and started jogging up the hill. It was pitch-black outside, and I stopped to catch my breath. That's when I saw it—a fresh cigarette lying on the ground, almost as if it had been placed there on purpose.

I froze, realizing I had a decision to make: pick it up and fall back into old habits, or keep going.

With tears streaming down my face, I ran up the hill at full speed, yelling as I went. I had done it—I had overcome. I was so proud of myself!

When we decide to move out of the way and let go of our excuses, we create room for God to work. When we choose to focus and discipline ourselves, we begin to see real results. Here are some practical steps I took to make room for Him:

Some Things I Did to Allow God to Move in My Life

- Stopped watching TV (I don't even own one anymore).
- Deleted social media apps from my phone until the Lord told me it was time to come out of hiding.
- Practiced celibacy.
- That process in that season of my life made one thing clear… **Girl, get out of His way!**
- Now it's your turn. Take a moment and ask yourself:
- What distractions are keeping you from God right now?
- What is one step you can take today to make more room for Him?

Once I cleared the distractions, the real battle showed up: me vs. me.

Surrender in the Boxing Ring

This victory wasn't just about quitting smoking—it was about the fight within. Do you ever feel like you're in a boxing ring while on your mission, constantly getting hit from all angles? Life keeps delivering uppercuts and punches to your chest, leaving you weak and vulnerable. You fight back as hard as possible, holding your own, standing firm. But with every hit, you feel yourself growing weaker and weaker. Your punches slow down, and you realize that even your best punch can't dent what you're facing.

Now you're on the boxing ring floor, and the referee begins to count down. You try to get up, but you can't feel your muscles. Fear and defeat creep in, whispering, "You'll never be good enough," "Just give up," "You'll never amount to anything." The referee is on number 6. You're overwhelmed: "Oh no, this is it. I'm a failure." At 7, you say, "I surrender," and suddenly you hear that familiar voice: "Mommy, we're going to make it to the top. You got this. It ain't over until God says it's over. The battle is not yours—it's the Lord's." By 8, you begin feeling your body again. You crawl on all fours, tears streaming, and you get a vision of all the people you've helped along the way. You remember you are needed and loved. At 9, you cry out, "Father, I can't do this on my own; I need Your help!" At 10, you're on your feet with hands raised in total surrender. Raising your hands signifies surrender it signifies victory

And that's where this all comes together. You've been given armor, you understand the battle, you know your purpose, you've faced distractions, you've seen God's hand The only question left is this: what will you do with it?

How Long Will You Wait?

How long will you wait for things to change? You were made for more than whatever you're settling for right now. God has given you a purpose—an assignment—and now it's time to rise and walk in it. Stop letting fear, distractions, and doubt hold you back. Creation waits for *you—*your story, your strength, and your voice. It's time to take action.

For years, you've been sitting on the ideas God has given you. Romans 8:19 says: The creation waits in eager expectation for the sons of God to be revealed. Whatever your story is, it will free someone.

The reason you survived—why the car accident didn't kill you, why the betrayal didn't destroy you—is because you were set apart to show someone else who may be enduring what God delivered you from. You can show them that the mountain can be moved. What an honor that God wants to use you. In fact, it has nothing to do with you, but it's all for His glory. –Galatians 2:20 says: For it is no longer I who live, but Christ that lives in me. Your world is waiting on you; your family is waiting for you; your community and city are waiting on you. Maybe your testimony will help a struggling teenager, a broken woman, someone who is battling sickness or your business idea will turn a dying community into a thriving one. You just never know what doors will open once you decide to just do it! The moment you put on that armor, use your weapons, and tap in—it's lights, camera, action. Now back to the process, in that season when I was learning to take up my cross…

MY THOUGHTS

115

CHAPTER SEVEN

Begin Again

My intention in giving my son away for a month—and taking up my cross—was to seek God's plan. However, when my son came home, I still had no plan. I lay on my bed, frustration rising like a storm, unsure of what to do next. I cried out to God, "You said, You know the plans You have for me, plans to prosper and not harm me. I don't even know where to begin, Lord!"

Suddenly, I heard Him say, "Start where you're at, with what you have." I was relieved when I received this command—it was like a lightbulb turning on. I realized I already had a lot of things my hands were tied to. "Oh yeah… I do have…," I thought.

> "Start where you're at, with what you have."

So I immediately grabbed a piece of cardboard and wrote down everything. As I listed each item, my heart began to lighten, and a sense of clarity and excitement filled me. Seeing my resources in writing made me realize I wasn't starting from scratch. This simple act shifted my perspective. Listen, sometimes you gotta remind God of what He said.

Action Step: Take Inventory

Sis, grab a piece of cardboard or paper right now.

I stopped focusing on what I lacked and began to see what I actually had. It felt like I'd been walking around with blinders on—That what happens when emotions take over. Writing things down proved far more powerful than letting my ideas roam around in my head.

I remember a conversation with my sis back in Michigan. She quoted Erykah Badu: "Write things down and watch them get real." One thing I wrote down that day changed everything. I realized I had already planted a seed I hadn't even recognized yet—**Embracing All of Me.**

Embracing All of Me was geared toward helping young ladies between the ages of 13–19 embrace their worth, foster self-confidence, and build a foundation of faith. They came from all walks of life and dealt with real struggles. Being their outlet—offering the help they needed—was an honor I did not take lightly. It takes more than just Mom and Dad; it truly takes a village.

Developing a teen group had always been a dream of mine. I remember being in eighth grade when my then-best friend, now my sister, ChaRae, and I said, "When we grow up, we're going to run a teen group and give young ladies what we didn't have growing up—a listening ear." And you know what? We actually did it! It didn't last as long as I thought it would, but we made it happen.

We held weekly sessions with the girls, discussing topics like forgiveness, identity, and knowing your worth. My desire was for them to be in spaces where these conversations were happening naturally so they wouldn't feel foreign as they grew older—much like the experience I had in a room full of positivity in my early twenties. I wanted them to have that experience much sooner so they knew who they are and whose they are.

We even held a special event called the Inward Beauty Workshop. We hosted this mini conference at the Marriott Hotel in Homestead, PA, with a guest speaker, and my son and nephews even performed a dance. It was truly amazing! Our goal was to cultivate a community where the girls felt safe, heard, and equipped with the tools they needed before stepping into adulthood.

One simple lesson we taught was keeping a personal care bag on hand. As a teen, I didn't know the importance of tracking your cycle or carrying backup supplies in case of an "accident." So we designed care bags with the girls, teaching them practical lessons on personal hygiene.

We went on field trips, created lasting memories, and shared stories. They even received certificates at the end of the program. Having this responsibility gave me fuel for where I was physically, spiritually, and emotionally. Those young ladies looked up to me, and I had to fight to show them something different. One of my girls said, "Miss Yas, you're the only person who ever cared and asked me how I was truly doing." That stuck with me. This wasn't just a program; this was our future—our now.

Their belief in what we were doing lit a fire in me. My vision expanded, and I started seeing how my coaching business could build on the foundation God was laying. Changing the narrative for the next generation—and the ones before us—had to start with me, with us, the ones called now. These young people didn't need someone to just talk; they needed someone to show up and be about it.

I remember teaching a class of teen boys and girls and asking, "Who here truly believes they are Kings and Queens?" I called them princes and princesses because they had to grow into royalty. Out of about 20 kids, none—zero—raised their hands.

So here's the reality: we tell them they're royalty, but are we actually treating them that way? Are we showing them what it looks like to walk in that authority, to hold themselves with that dignity? That moment hit me like a lightning bolt—I wasn't just going to tell them; I was going to show them. Every day, in every interaction. None of that "do as I say, not as I do"—yeah, that thinking was not it!

The foundation of Embracing All of Me became the seed from which my coaching business would grow. I learned so much from working with those girls—mainly about the simplicity of community and holding space for one another. These lessons became the cornerstone of Striving for His Excellence. Honestly, I got the name Striving for His Excellence from my spiritual father. Originally, I had "Risen from the Ground" in mind for the company, and at another time it was "I Love Me Out Loud"—remember that self-love and positive affirmations phase I was in. I've been working at this for a while now. I believe I once asked my spiritual father for a letter of recommendation, and he ended that letter with, "Striving in and for His Excellence." Months or years later, I was doodling and realized that name just clicked. I phoned my spiritual father, asked if I could use it, and he gave me his blessing.

Striving for His Excellence exists to serve women by helping them embrace their identity and worth, break generational barriers, and dismantle negative belief systems through the Word of God. Our mission is to empower women to step fully into who God created them to be.

Here's just a taste of what we do to make that happen:

- Personal development that equips you to lead your life with purpose
- Practical life skills to navigate everyday challenges with confidence
- One-on-one coaching sessions to help you clarify your path and goals
- Women's retreats designed to refresh your spirit and deepen your faith
- And so much more!

Every session, every workshop, every conversation is built to help you rise, shine, and live the life God has for you. Striving for His Excellence is a place where we walk alongside one another in brokenness, wholeness, ups and downs.

The It's Time to Get Up women's conference would be our first major project for the company—the same conference God placed in my heart and called me to do in Chapter 4. Where there is no vision, the people perish. –Proverbs 29:18

The ultimate goal is to have a building for Striving for His Excellence—a for-profit business. The revenue from this business—through merchandise, speaking engagements, workshops, and retreats—would support our nonprofit ministry, Embracing All of Me. This approach allows the ministry to flourish without relying solely on donations while also providing opportunities to expand our reach and impact.

I already had my LLC, a website, and business cards. I had everything I needed to get started, so I became innovative: turning my dining room into an office. My dining table became my desk, and I set up a backdrop, ring lights, and cameras. I had all the tools to launch both the for-profit and the ministry, using one to sustain the other and move both forward.

Use What You Have / Write It Down

I'll bet that if you checked your own inventory, you too already have everything you need to start. What has God told you to do? Its time to finish it!

Take Inventory

Grab that piece of cardboard or paper from earlier and take a moment now to list five resources in your toolbox—whether it's time, skills, or people.

I had no clue what I was going to say. I felt so inadequate, unsure how I could possibly get in front of a camera or speak to people and say anything that would encourage them in that season of my life.

One day, while scrolling on Pinterest, I came across Exodus 4:10: I, the Lord, will give you the words to speak. Even though the Lord was showing me what I needed to do, I still had doubts. Yes, I wanted to encourage people, show them they weren't alone, but I was shook to speak up. Seeing this scripture clarified that God was listening. He will communicate with you in ways only you can understand. The question is: are you listening?

Consistency Is Key

When He told me to start with what I had and start now, that's exactly what I did. Every morning, I'd wake up early and worship Him with the song He's Preparing Me by Daryl Coley, put on that full armor like I told y'all, throw on some workout gear, and head to my living room. Before stepping onto my rug, I'd remind myself to take off my shoes, for this is holy ground –Exodus 3:5. Then I'd magnify and exalt the Father before asking Him for anything. I'd lay out my daily plans before Him and ask that He reveal His plan instead. Honestly, the key to starting was including Him in it all.

During that time, I had to remain focused. Like anything else, I treated my Father's business as if I were working for man. Even without a large following, I had plenty of contacts in my phone, so I used what I had: my voice, my heart. I would send messages I believed the Lord was prompting me to share with the women in my contacts.

One woman said a message I sent gave her the strength to face a difficult decision that day. Another shared that it was "right on time" for where she was, telling me, "I'll never forget you, and I'm definitely cheering you on." Yet another sister said, "I'd turned off my phone all week—life was crazy—and then I turned it on to see messages from you! Exactly what I needed." For some, I even prayed with them, developing closer bonds simply by being available sharing His Word and loving on His people. That's women empowering and supporting one another through a simple "hello." Do not despise the day of small things –Zechariah 4:10.

When I sent those messages, I was also talking to myself. I've adopted the mindset that if I'm growing through something, someone else is too. I learned I could help others grow while still being a work in progress. Instead of focusing on me, it became about helping us.

A generous person will prosper; whoever refreshes others will be refreshed –Proverbs 11:25.

So, for those who think you need to have it all together, you don't. Put your trust in God and have faith, even if it's as small as a mustard seed –Matthew 17:20–21. Yolanda Adams' Never Give Up says it best: "It's all inside of you; you have everything you need, so keep the dream alive and don't let it die… Don't ever give up on you."

You can achieve that thing in your heart—if you couldn't, the desire wouldn't be so strong. Delight yourself in the Lord and He will give you the desires of your heart –Psalm 37:4.

After sending these messages, I started posting actionable videos on Instagram. Even though I'm not considered part of the "popular bunch," I started anyway, aiming to make an impact because justice was going to be served. Listen, sis: I don't care if nobody shows—you show up. Whatever He called and gave you to do, baby girl, it is needed.

In the Wilderness

Mind you, I did all this in the wilderness. That "wilderness" felt like a desert of isolation, with no clear direction. My heart ached in the silence, unsure where I was headed. The "shallow place" wasn't just a lack of depth; it was emptiness. But it was in that place I found a deeper connection with God, like a seed waiting to sprout in barren soil. The wilderness is a setup, and it's necessary. In my opinion, the wilderness is where God isolates you so you learn to look within. Even though it feels like your life is falling apart, it's actually coming together. At first, you think it's over for you. Little did I know He was about to bless me with a grant to keep moving forward!

The Grant

I was so focused on using what I had and seeking out His will for my life that I totally forgot about the grant money—until I received an email saying it had finally come through! I burst into tears of joy, overwhelmed by God's provision. When I tell you God's timing is unmatched, I mean it! I had been moving forward in obedience without knowing where the next provision would come from. I had made peace with starting small, using what I had, and trusting that He would provide when the time was right.

And here it was—the very thing I wasn't even thinking about anymore—showing up just when I needed it most. God was showing me that when I stay faithful to the work, He stays faithful to His promises. I felt He was giving me the next steps: it was time to look for a venue for the It's Time to Get Up Conference.

Call to Action / Check Your Inventory

By now, you've probably realized—you already have what you need to start. You've taken inventory, trusted God with what's in your hands, and learned that small steps still move you forward. Now it's about obedience and momentum.

So, what happens when you actually use what He's given you? When you take that faith step and give it back to Him? That's when God begins to multiply your little into much.

Can you guess what I used the grant money for? Stay tuned to find out how this grant shaped everything going forward.

MY THOUGHTS

126

CHAPTER EIGHT

Your Will Be Done

Remember how I was praying for an increase in my finances? Well, let me tell you—God really did His big one for your girl! I couldn't believe it when I actually received the $10,000 grant. Earlier in the year, I'd gotten a letter saying I was approved, but when it came time to access the funds, it felt like I was running through loops and hoops. So, when I finally got that email confirming the upload, the timing couldn't have been more perfect.

Of course, I was elated! What a relief to know I could catch up on bills and buy a van for Embracing All of Me, with the remaining amount covering the venue for the "It's Time to Get Up Women Conference 2023." Or so I thought.

Decisions, Decisions

Earlier, I shared my fear of becoming homeless you know, when I got the flat tire. Well I was also $3,000 in debt behind on bills. Praying desperately for a breakthrough. And then—BOOM. I received that email stating we got the grant, Problem solved! I used some of it to pay off those debts and to keep my bills current. I could have used what was left for a down payment on a vehicle for Embracing all of me, but I knew, deep down, God wanted me to use those funds for His Temple. I chose to invest in the "It's Time to Get Up Women Conference" instead.

It was a tough decision because Embracing All of Me was my "baby," and having a vehicle would help transport the girls. However, I also sensed this calling was bigger than even the conference—this was my destiny. I was done doing things my way.

Finding the Temple (Venue Search)

It was time to call the lady God chose to help organize the conference. We prayed together, agreeing that our first step was to find a suitable venue, which I referred to as the "temple."

First Venue

The first place we visited was beautiful but far too small for the vision we had.

Second Venue

We moved on to the second venue, and it was gorgeous. A stunning entrance, all the necessary equipment, and a price well within our budget. We were thrilled! This was it, we thought, so we booked it on the spot.

Initially, we hoped to host the event in September 2022, but those dates were taken. We also worried about busy months ahead with the holidays. So, we settled on January 2023—a fresh start for the new year. But as we debated, uncertainty crept in: Was January the right time? Should we stick to the original plan?

Sitting in the parking lot, we discussed our next move. We had walked boldly thus far, but now, we didn't know what to do. So, we prayed. Then I opened my Bible to the book of Haggai—the same book God first led me to, along with Zechariah, when He asked me to rebuild His home/temple. And there it was, in bold letters: "In the ninth month, the temple was restored." We began to shout, realizing that in God's timing, the temple would be ready by January 2023. It clicked. Nine months, like the full term of pregnancy. We felt we were carrying His child, wanting to give birth in His timing and for His glory.

If we hadn't stopped to pray, we wouldn't have known what to do next. The Bible tells us our steps are ordered, but we often get caught up trying to figure it all out, failing to act at all. Prayer is action. With every step, our confidence grew. We knew—God was with us, leading the way.

We contacted the event center and reserved January 14, 2023, as our date. We paid $2,000 without delay. I used the grant money for gas, equipment, and food during our team meet-ups. To cover remaining costs, we planned to seek donations and write proposal letters. I'd hoped to use the rest of the grant for a van for Embracing All of Me.

On One Accord

Once the venue was set, we turned to God again for guidance on the next steps. We prayed more—mornings and evenings—and sought our wise mentors for counsel. –1 Corinthians 12:12–27.

So not only did we ensure we were in harmony as a team with Christ, but we also made sure we were individually on the same page with Him. I joined various prayer lines and attended Bible studies. We remained vigilant.

Third Time's a Charm

When we revisited the second venue, we realized it was too small. So we tried one last place—a beautiful wedding venue the lady I was called to work with had in mind.

Final Venue

This time, we dressed in our finest, like the daughters of the King. It's vital to carry yourself with dignity, no matter where you are—valley or mountaintop—because your Father is King. When you look good, you feel good, and when you feel good, you move differently.

Ask the Holy Spirit to teach you how to walk, talk, and dress like Him. I'd gotten so good at this, I'd even ask the Lord what He wanted me to wear. I take my life—no longer mine—very seriously, and trust me, He has taste. Start dressing up for Him, shining for His glory, and guess what? You automatically benefit.

As we stepped into the space, it came to life. One of my visions was to make women feel like they were entering a royal palace. We are God's children, so we are royal -1 Peter 2:9. These women came from brokenness, hurt, and pain; it was vital they experienced God like never before. The idea was for us to walk into His palace—His holy temple—knowing this was where we belonged with Him, even if just for one day.

This place had everything. It was intimate and beautiful, with full setup and tear-down services. We didn't want to leave, we were so in awe. Suddenly, I felt the need to pray. That's how we knew our search to rebuild the Lord's home was over. The other two venues were nice, but we didn't pray at either of them.

When we walked into this building, we fell to our knees and went to war in prayer. The noise around us faded as we encountered God's powerful presence.

After leaving, my partner and I were amazed and decided to cancel the other venue, retrieving our down payment. We then put $1,000 toward the wedding venue—His "temple." Looking back, it truly was the Lord's temple: a wedding venue representing the Church (Christ's Bride), opening His temple for His daughters—His brides—to get back up again.

After making that $1,000 investment toward rebuilding the temple, we had $4,000 left from the grant. Our original plan was to raise the rest of the conference money via grants and sponsorships, but for some reason, this plan didn't pan out.

Wrestling with God

Now I had to make a choice. Should I use the money for the conference or buy a vehicle for Embracing All of Me?

I was unemployed, with limited income. Part of me wanted the van for Ubering and running the girls' group, generating some income while I prepared for the event. It made sense on paper. But after two weeks of fighting and praying, God broke through. I didn't just struggle—I fought. I fought with myself, with logic, with fear, and even with God. "Lord, this doesn't make sense! Why would You bless me with this grant just to have me give it back, I have a whole child to take care of, bills to pay. I need this!" My voice cracked as I wiped away tears of frustration and confusion. I felt torn—like I was being asked to sacrifice the little I had left. But wasn't this the very thing I had prayed for? "I trust You," I told the Lord, barely believing it myself. But—I wasn't really trusting Him yet. I was still holding on to my will and my way, afraid to let go.

Eventually I came to grips with at the end of the day, it was all His. so, I told Him Lord, not my will but Yours. If You're asking me to lay this down, I will. In that moment, peace found me. I cried, fought with myself, and wrestled with Him—until I realized I'd learned enough lessons, and I wanted to prove to the Lord I was fully committed. It was no longer about convenience; it was about honoring His will. This was a true "not my will, but Yours" moment.

Many are the plans in a person's heart, but it is the Lord's purpose that prevails. –Proverbs 19:21

I'm All In

I called my conference partner—whom God had paired with me for this assignment—and shared the news: I was going to put $4,000 down on the wedding venue, His temple. I sat there, staring at the confirmation page. My heart was RACING—90 on the freeway. At this point, I was squeezing in farts, about to risk it all! Lord, have mercy. My hand hovered over the payment button. This was it, no turning back. The money would be gone—no safety net, no security, no fallback plan. Just faith. I exhaled, whispering, "God, you're going to have to catch me. My mind screamed at me to wait, to think it over, to play it safe. With one last deep breath, and a big gulp, the card was swiped. The screen refreshed. Payment confirmed. And just like that—I was all in.

A sense of peace flooded my chest. "Alright, Lord," I said. "Now, it's on You. Together, we booked it, which included everything we needed: setup, tear-down, decorations, breakfast, and dinner. It was a relief to know those logistical details were handled, letting us focus entirely on the vision God placed in our hearts.

$4,000 plus the $1,000 we already put it in may seem small to some, but it was major for me. This was the greatest financial investment I'd ever made—a leap of faith symbolizing me betting on myself and the vision God gave me.

As you move toward living for Him or becoming your best self, celebrate every step. Lisa Nichols says, "What gets celebrated gets repeated." Don't get so focused on the destination that you miss the beauty of the process. Find joy in small victories and praise Him even while waiting. –Philippians 4:11–12.

> Celebrate every step.

After making the investment, we took a moment to celebrate—it felt good! That celebration wasn't just for us; it was an act of gratitude to God for leading us this far.

Reflect

What small victories deserve celebration today?
How can you express gratitude right now?

Later that same day, I attended a two-day women's event titled "Power Up—Faith Through It All." I hadn't planned on going, but since this was my first time organizing such a large event, volunteering at someone else's conference seemed invaluable for behind-the-scenes experience—a humbling opportunity I couldn't pass up.

Although I was there to assist, I found myself drawn to a gospel concert happening in one of the rooms. So I decided to go be a little nosey. Honestly, I thought the speaking engagement was that night, but it was actually scheduled for the next day. I asked one of the women in charge if I could sit in, and she welcomed me in with a smile.

As I immersed myself in worship, a song called "I Am All In" by Maranda Curtis began to play. I'd never heard it before, but the moment it started, I was overwhelmed by God's presence. The lyrics spoke directly to where I was in my journey, and as the song ministered to my heart, the Holy Spirit reassured me that He saw me.

I wasn't even supposed to be in that room, but that song—whew—it was right on time. There's a quote that says, "Where words fail, music speaks." At that moment, I knew I'd made the right move. God was showing me that I was exactly where He wanted me to be—right in the middle of His will.

Finding Worship Leaders / Fellowshipping with Various Congregations

The next step was finding worship leaders for the It's Time to Get Up Women Conference. Inspired by the power of worship I'd just experienced, we began looking for the vessels God would use to lead others into His Glory. We visited different churches, each with unique styles and communities.

- Homestead Church: Unexpectedly, we were blessed with intercessors who prayed, fasted, and supported us. I remain connected with them to this day. Stepping out in faith gave us relationships and spiritual support we didn't realize we needed.

- Hill District Church: So many young adults on fire for God. Coming from a more "seasoned" congregation, I wasn't used to seeing peers my age so hungry for Him. It was truly invigorating.
- Downtown Pittsburgh Church: This church wasn't located downtown but between the hill and downtown Pittsburgh. The location was what made this church so unique. It was set up where you knew God was reclaiming that territory!

This process taught me an invaluable lesson: as believers, we should not confine our fellowship just to our home churches. I am not saying to eat at everyone's table—some folks don't wash their hands before cooking, and some do not preach sound doctrine—so knowing the Word for yourself is crucial. Still, there's freedom in God, and we are not limited to one style of worship.

Despite all our efforts, the search continued. We did not find our worship leader just then, but God gave us something even greater: a strengthened spiritual foundation.

Strengthened Prayer Life

My prayer life went from mundane to vibrant. I participated in prayer calls, attended Bible studies, and prayed with strangers on buses, everywhere I went the Lord would cause me to pray with those in need. Prayer became my second language. I lived out the verse Pray without ceasing –1 Thessalonians 5:17. My focus shifted entirely to the Kingdom of God and His purposes, and He increased my compassion for His people.

This transformation opened doors I never saw coming. I visited hospitals to pray for patients, witnessed miracles, and encountered God's power in extraordinary ways. It was a season of growth and surrender, a time where I truly embraced the call to intercede for others and seek our land's healing –Matthew 10. Each step reinforced this truth: when you move in obedience, God provides.

> When you move in obedience, God provides.

MY THOUGHTS

✝

CHAPTER NINE

Courage in the Face of Fear

A Test of Faith

Sometimes, our faith needs to be tested—not to show how powerful we are, but to demonstrate how powerful He is. God wants to see if we truly believe. I just never thought I would be tested like this.

One of My Favorite Quotes

We delight in the beauty of the butterfly, but rarely admit the changes it has gone through to achieve that beauty –Maya Angelou

Much like when we see someone successful in person or on social media, we often forget the sacrifices they made to get there. We might envy someone's achievements without realizing what it cost them. This is why I love hearing people's stories—if my journey is interesting, I know yours is too. And witnessing—or hearing about—a caterpillar becoming a butterfly never ceases to amaze me!

As we were praying and preparing for the "It's Time to Get Up" women's conference, I had an unexpected encounter that reminded me just how real this spiritual life aint nothing to play with.

One night, I was lying in bed, casually scrolling through Facebook, when I received a message notification from supposedly Marvin Sapp! I couldn't believe it. He greeted me with a kind message, wishing blessings upon my family. I was thrilled but also skeptical, so I did some digging to confirm it was truly him. After checking his page and live recordings—sure enough, this was the real Marvin Sapp at least it appeared that way! I couldnt help but wonder, what was God up to now?

Disclaimer: I later realized it may not have been the real Marvin Sapp—but in that moment, it sure felt like God was using even that to get my attention.

Reflecting on Single Motherhood

During the early stages of my life, being a single mother was absolute hell. However, two songs helped me through those dark times. One was Father, Can You Hear Me? by Tamela Mann. I sang it all day and night while rocking my son to sleep. I didn't have a relationship with God then; actually, I was angry with Him. Little did I know I was singing to Him the whole time.

By the time my son turned two or three, I decided I had enough. I was ready for an upgrade in my life. I was searching for something new. That's when I found a Marvin Sapp CD. The first track, "I Believe," was something nice. In fact, the entire album was great, but that first track—babyyyyyy—was extra special!

After a long day at business school—studying to become a paralegal I would pick my son up from my sisters house, go home, roll a blunt, and play "I Believe" on repeat. Sometimes I cried; other times I was grooving to it. That song carried me into the next phase of life, planting seeds of faith before I ever acknowledged God. I didn't know Him, but He sure knew me!

God Speaks in Personal Ways

God has a unique way of capturing our attention—through a favorite song, a random social media post, a billboard, a dream, or even a Facebook message. He knows how to reach each of us, so we need to stay alert. Now, I know you're curious about my conversation with supposedly Marvin Sapp, so let me dive in.

Facebook Messages

I was super geeked when I thought Marvin Sapp hit me up on Facebook. We exchanged several messages; he encouraged me to let God work in my life, reminding me that the Lord was doing miraculous things for me. I told him about the Women's conference, and he was praying on our behalf. He asked about my line of work, saying the Holy Spirit had nudged him to pray for me. In my head I was like, "The Holy Spirit told you to pray for little ol' me? Of all the people in the world?"

After I shared my work, our conversation ended. Although we'd been texting back and forth for a while, I felt disappointed when he stopped responding. Honestly, I worried he might think my calling was crazy—but I realize now that was my own insecurity talking.

A Message of Warning

Later that morning, while I was running late to take my son to school, Marvin Sapp responded again. We were waiting at the bus stop, and seeing his name pop up definitely brightened my commute with my boy. I was excited when who I thought was Marvin Sapp said he admired what I did for work. Then he declared:

"God will suddenly terminate the appointment of everyone frustrating you in your place of work and grant you success in the name of Jesus."

I replied, "Amen. Have a fabulous day." At the time, his words seemed random, but looking back, I see now—he was warning me. I was about to step into a battle. It's funny how God will send a word or some kind of warning before the storm comes. He is so balm like that. Of course if your anything like me, we dont never recognize it until after the fact. Lol always gotta learn the hard way smh, annoying… Stay with me. I am going somewhere…

Stranger Things

I ran into an acquaintance who offered us a ride to the bus stop, which was unusual for us. While waiting, I noticed a strange man nearby but didn't think much of it. Once the bus arrived, there were only a few passengers: me, my son, a couple of other people, and this strange man. As we approached downtown, the driver announced he couldn't go any further—some issue—so we all had to get off at the same stop.

The Strange Man Follows

As my son and I walked toward his school, I realized this strange man was following us. My heart pounded; I felt scared and unsure of what to do. Oddly enough, there wasn't a person in sight. Not even any cars I could flag down. I was shook, wondering how I would protect my son through all of it. The only thing there was to do was pray. I gripped my son's hand tighter, As I greeted the man to break the ice, asking if he was okay. He said he wasn't. His words were slurred, and I couldn't understand him. I asked his name—he said, "Straggler." Then I offered to pray for him, but he declined. I said "okay" and wished him well.

No One in Sight

My son whispered, "Is that man following us?" I said yes and told him to pray, pleading the blood of Jesus and rebuking the devil. We reached the end of the street, but it was a green light with cars speeding by. The cars flew so fast I couldn't even try to stop one. Boldly, we jetted across the street, not even thinking about the risk of getting hit—desperate to escape that man. But guess what? He crossed too, ignoring the danger of oncoming traffic. It was surreal.

Am I Tripping?

My stomach dropped. I yanked my son's hand tighter, my mind racing. This man wasn't just walking—he was mirroring us. I zig-zagged to see if I was imagining it—he zig-zagged too. It was wild. This was real. I was looking for an escape, but where? There were no people, like I said before, the cars weren't slowing down. It was literally just me and my son and the man. It was like a scene straight out of a nightmare. I spotted a hotel we usually pass and darted inside, telling the security guard a man was following us. The guard told the man to head in the opposite direction.

Help Is on the Way

The security guard reassured me that the man had gone another way and told us to exit through the back. My son and I paused to pray in the hallway before leaving. I asked if he still wanted to go to school—he said yes. I was amazed by his courage; I expected him to want a mental health day. I know I needed one, but he was determined to attend class.

We walked toward the school, and for a moment, the coast was clear. Suddenly, my son looked back and saw the strange man again.

Shout-Out to the School Staff

Praying in my head, "Lord, help us." As we frantically rushed into the school. Thankfully, the door locked behind us. And guess what? The man had the nerve to try to get into the building. Staff members escorted us to another room. I feared for my son, though he seemed calmer than me. Just so you know, its easy to say what you would do in a situation until you're actually in it.

The police arrived soon after. I explained everything, but the man claimed he'd mistaken the school for a fire or police station. His slurred speech alarmed the staff and the officer, but nothing more could be done. Looking back, it's remarkable that a security guard was at the hotel and the school—and the police showed up. We were clearly protected; God's Goshen was over us. I was too caught up in the moment to recognize His hand.

The Kid Has Guts

I asked my son if he wanted to finish the school day or come home. After all that, this lil' dude still wanted to stay. I was astonished; the whole situation overwhelmed me, yet he found the courage to keep going. What a brave kid! I gave him a big hug, told him I loved him, and went on my way. The police officer offered to drive me home, but I chose to stay downtown to work near my son's school.

The Aftermath

I felt vulnerable and weak, craving comfort. My dad lived in Philadelphia at the time; so it made no sense to call him. My mom was at work, and I didn't want to freak her out. I tried one of my mentors but no answer. Finally, I called my spiritual father.

Support from My Spiritual Father

Hearing his voice, I instantly began to cry, explaining the incident. He assured me I did the right thing but confirmed what occurred was a spiritual attack. The name "Straggler" means to strangle or choke—the man was sent to inject fear, hoping I'd abandon the calling God gave me.

He reminded me we wrestle not against flesh and blood but against principalities in high places –Ephesians 6:12. Essentially, it wasn't just the man—it was his spirit. The thief comes to steal, kill, and destroy –John 10:10. The enemy recognized God's moving power in us and wanted to choke out the promise.

Stand Firm on His Word

My spiritual father instructed me to repeat two scriptures aloud:

1. God has not given me the spirit of fear, but of power, love, and a sound mind. –2 Timothy 1:7

2. Trust in the Lord with all your heart; do not lean on your own understanding. In all your ways acknowledge Him, and He will direct your path. –Proverbs 3:5

The Woman, the Dragon, and Her Son

Later that day, while I was at home scrolling on Pinterest, I stumbled on Revelation 12, titled "The Woman, the Dragon, and Her Son." In that chapter, a dragon tries to devour a male child the moment he's born. –Revelation 12:1–4. Though I wasn't carrying Jesus, I was carrying His baby—the conference. The enemy's mission was to choke it out, to plant fear so I would quit.

We must realize we'll face opposition when fulfilling God's will. Our fight isn't physical but mighty through God. We can't fight every spirit or sense of inferiority alone; we need the Holy Spirit to fight for us. We strengthen our faith by fasting, praying, thanking God, and speaking His Word. He's not a man that He should lie—He keeps every promise.

We must wear the full armor of God which we've discussed in chapter 6, praying continuously in the Spirit -Ephesians 6:18. As my son demonstrated, we need courage in the face of fear. Don't back out because you sense an attack. He's already shown you how to navigate while giving you the tools. If you've been going in circles, maybe you're spiritually naked—it's time, woman of God, to put on your armor.

Facing Fear Head-On: A Quick Guide

Sometimes, we find ourselves in unexpected moments—just like I did with the strange man following me. Fear can ambush us so quickly our hearts race, our minds blank, and we feel powerless. Here's a short guide of practical steps for when fear tries to shake you up.

*Please note this deals more with spiritual attacks than purely physical ones.

1. Just Breathe
   - Before you react, take a slow, deep breath. Fear makes us panic, but a single breath can calm nerves and refocus. Be still and know that I am God. –Psalm 46:10
2. There Is Power in the Name of Jesus
   - Just His name alone is all the power you need to trample the enemy, just say JESUS
   - I sought the Lord, and he answered me; he delivered me from all my fears. –Psalm 34:4
3. Remember God's Word
   - Scriptures like 2 Timothy 1:7 or Psalm 91 can be lifesaving. Declare them: "God has not given me fear—I have power, love, and a sound mind!"
4. Assess Your Surroundings
   - If there's immediate danger (like I faced), look for a safe place: a lobby, a store, a security guard. God often provides an escape route; remain alert.
   - The name of the Lord is a strong tower; the righteous run to it and are safe. –Proverbs 18:10
5. Reach Out for Help
   - If possible, call a prayer partner, mentor, or spiritual leader. Sharing your situation with someone who prays helps break fear's grip.

- For where two or three gather in my name, there am I with them. –Matthew 18:20

6. Speak Against Fear

- Fear thrives in secrecy. Declare: "I will not be afraid; the Lord is with me!" This shifts your mindset.

- "Resist the devil, and he will flee from you." –James 4:7

7. Take Courageous Action

- Courage doesn't mean feeling no fear; it means moving forward despite it. Like my son deciding to stay at school.

- "I am not facing this alone. God goes before me." –Deuteronomy 31:8

> Courage doesn't mean feeling no fear; it means moving forward despite it.

Reflection

Fear can overwhelm us in a heartbeat, but it doesn't have the final say. Every time you confront fear with prayer, Scripture, and practical steps, you weaken its hold. It's okay if your heart still pounds and your hands shake—God's power isn't lessened by your human reactions. By pausing, praying, and reaching out, you're reminding fear it has no permanent home in your mind or spirit. God's perfect love drives out fear –1 John 4:18. Never underestimate the strength of even the smallest act of faith in a fearful situation.

Final Text with Marvin Sapp

Later that evening, Marvin Sapp messaged me again, asking if I believed in God's miracles performed that day. I just looked at my phone, realizing the Lord was surely with me and this assignment, this conference; was going to be big!

Job's Trials / Our Trials

In the book of Job, God and Satan discuss Job's faithfulness. Satan believes Job would curse God if his wealth and blessings were stripped away. Ultimately, God grants the enemy permission to taunt Job, fully confident His son will pass the test –Job 1:6–12.

Sometimes we blame the devil for every hardship, but perhaps you did nothing wrong; you're growing through these things because God trusts you to remain faithful. He knows you will pass the test.

All these difficult situations like Marvin Sapp's warning and my encounter with the strange man are meant to bring us closer to God. Often, we don't see it, so He shakes us a little to open our eyes. I'm not too certain if that was the real Marvin Sapp or not maybe it wasn't but like I mentioned before, He knows how to stir us up. When life starts shaking, it might mean you're doing something right! In fact, that fire, those trials, that pressing, might actually help someone else break loose.

Stay strong, because the assignment God gave you requires preparation. Thankfully, He's gracious enough to prepare us. Keep pressing forward praying, fasting, working. If you don't quit, your reward awaits. You've come too far for God to leave you, and the outcome will be better than you can imagine –Deuteronomy 31:6–8, Joshua 1:6–9.

The Mission Didn't Change

I once read a quote:

"I asked God, 'Why are You taking me through troubled waters?' He replied, 'Because your enemies can't swim.'"

Deep! While building His temple, my partner and I fell out of sync. The same woman God instructed me to partner with to host the its time to get up women's conference. We weren't praying together as much; she was busy with other God-given tasks, which I understood, but I also felt, "If we're going to do this, let's do it. If not, let me know." I knew this was my assignment, and I wasn't stopping for no one.

The Bit and Bridle

Feeling uneasy, I called my first lady. She shared an analogy about a horse and rider: the bit in the horse's mouth is painful, yet it keeps the horse on track. Ignoring the rider's reins risks a ditch. Similarly, God holds the reins of our hearts. Yes, it can hurt to follow, but if we refuse, life's difficulties multiply. He sees the road ahead and wants to spare us needless pain.

Not everyone God places in your life is meant to be with you permanently; some are only there for a season.

When God Says Move, You Move

After praying and waiting, I finally spoke to my conference partner. She said she couldn't keep building God's temple with me. She disagreed about how often we should meet for prayer, believing morning and evening was excessive, and she felt uneasy about certain conference details. I was hurt by what she said, but I accepted this turn of events.

NOTE: When you feel uncomfortable and need to address a situation, don't tackle it head-on without guidance. Seek God's direction first. Go to wise counsel—someone who'll offer pearls of wisdom and not push you toward self-destruction. Had I not gone to the Lord before confronting my partner, I might've acted in my flesh and lost a good connection altogether. I wouldn't have been able to see things clearly or still hold gratitude for her.

People may say your dreams are too big or that you lack what it takes. They might question your faith, insisting God never called you to such a thing. But those are their own limitations, not yours. You know what God spoke—so keep moving. Continue praying, wishing them well with a genuine heart.

I've realized people aren't just blessings; they're gifts. I thank God for that wonderful woman and the season she served in my life. She was a friend I needed, gave me confidence to start, and opened doors through her connections—just like Abraham and Lot parting ways. When God says it's time to move, you move!

Remember, those who leave are simply fulfilling their part in the building process. God is the one who orchestrates the removal. As you keep going remember He is in the details and your steps are ordered. When people leave its all apart of His plan.

"I asked God, 'Why are You taking me through troubled waters?' He replied, 'Because your enemies can't swim.'" –Unknown

Acceptance / Next Steps

I was utterly discouraged initially, wondering if I'd misheard the Lord about putting on the conference. Yes, I know we'd sacrificed and endured so much, but that doubt still crept in. So, I stayed home a few days, feeling down, grieving what I'd pictured it might be. Once I felt strong enough to stand again—though still not feeling it I decided to head downtown for some fresh air.

I called my mom to complain some more. To my surprise she gave me sound advice this time: "Maybe God isn't changing the mission; He's just sending someone else. Don't stop doing what you're doing." I'm not used to my mom dropping pearls of wisdom, so her telling me that really encouraged me.

God is in the details, right? I didn't realize there was a festival going on downtown, but seeing all those vendors and tables, I was ready for the next phase of building His temple (conference) But here's what really got me: I wasn't even supposed to be downtown that day. He knew exactly where I needed to be. I didn't have to search for the right people; He literally dropped them right in my lap. When I say you don't have to chase what's meant for you? THIS was proof yet, AGAIN!

My next task was to find vendors for the conference. I made several contacts that day. A woman from the For His Glory prayer line who lived outside of my jurisdiction gave me a call that day. She said she got my number from the minister (my mentor) of the prayer line and felt led to connect with me. We prayed, and I told her all about what God was doing and getting ready to do. She was exactly what I needed, an event planner who specializes in women's events. That's just like God, though.

Let me tell you something: you don't have to hunt down what the Lord has for you. When the time is right, it'll literally come looking for you. Our job is to wait and focus on what's already in front of us.

MY THOUGHTS

CHAPTER TEN

Financial Freedom

When my conference partner and I went our separate ways, I couldn't see how the conference would come together. How was I going to do this on my own? I thought. To make matters worse, I was out of funds again, and my son's 10th birthday was coming up. Ten is a big deal, and to not have anything for him would've been insane. Keep in mind, I wasn't working—at least not traditionally. I was either going to trust God to do His thing, or I was going to panic.

Well, let's just say I did both. I panicked first, then I trusted. You know how we do. I won't go into major detail about how my son's 10th birthday turned out, but I will say this: the Lord did exceedingly, abundantly beyond what I could've ever imagined.

One of the hardest parts about walking with God is depending on Him and understanding that He will come through. It's easy to say "God will provide" when the fridge is full and the bills are paid—but what about when it's not? Well, that's a whole different ball game. And this was another one of those moments for me.

It's funny, because no matter how many times He has come through and shown Himself faithful, the moment I'm in need, I suddenly get amnesia—as if He's never made a way before. That's why it's so important to read and study the Word. Our flesh is still our flesh, and no matter how saved you think you are, it wants control -Romans 7:21-25. When the flesh takes over, we are left in our feelings and emotions, allowing how we feel to distort how we see our circumstances rather than standing on the truth.

We don't just study when times are hard—we fill up on the Word of God daily. At least that should be our posture. When we consistently feed on the Word of God, we strengthen our spirit man—and feeding our spirit daily ensures that when the flesh tries to rise, it won't stand a chance.

In other words, we who claim Jesus as our Lord and Savior must believe Him to do all things. Otherwise, we are no better than those who do not believe—those who see Him through the eyes of religion rather than relationship.

No matter the circumstance, we must "call those things which are not as though they were" -Romans 4:17, KJV. Because we who believe live by what? We live by faith! -Romans 1:17. As the church folk say, "He may not come when you want Him to, but He is always on time."

How He cared for me

You're probably wondering how I was able to get by and manage my everyday needs while I "wasn't working traditionally." I put air quotes around "wasn't," because most people believe that if you're not clocking in to a 9–5, you must not be busy. But baby, sitting at the feet of Jesus is work. Interceding and being available for Him to use you however He wants to—that's work. You are literally slaying dragons and breaking chains in the spirit. If that ain't work, I don't know what is.

The truth is, you don't even realize how much work you're putting in until you look back. Learning and being taught by the Master is work. Just because I was home and not clocking in the way others do, don't think I wasn't clocked in. Taking care of home and providing a peaceful atmosphere for my family—that's work too.

Now that we've cleared that up, here's the reality: during the time of preparation to set the captives free and rebuild His temple (aka the It's Time to Get Up Conference), God was my provider in very real ways. I received food stamps to feed my family. I also received a letter from my rental office stating that my rent would be $0 moving forward. The Lord is so dope—I wasn't even expecting that! Before I could begin to worry and wonder how I was going to make ends meet, the letter had already been sent. He knows what you need before you do –Matthew 6:8.

But the lump sum of grant money I mentioned in the previous chapter was gone, and the bills started piling up again. Having experienced that freedom of not having to worry, it was always a tug-of-war whether or not I should go back to work. I knew God had my back, but remember—He works on His time, and His time and mine don't always match up. It wasn't that I was lazy or didn't want to earn money for me and my boy; it just felt like I was moving backwards every time I even considered it. And trust me, I would get frustrated—because let's be honest, we as women are going to "get it done" regardless. But God challenged that kind of thinking every single time.

Who likes to walk around broke? Me—said no one ever!

So in those moments when I needed toiletry items or something extra, I would literally say, "Okay Lord, okay Daddy—I need this amount of money. How are we going to pay for it?" He always answered. Sometimes He placed someone on my heart to ask for help, and they would give with no hesitation. Other times, someone would randomly call and tell me to send my CashApp. And sometimes, a babysitting gig would show up right when I needed it most.

Like a sheep listening to the Shepherd, I followed His instructions. When He said drink, I'd drink. When He said go, I'd go. If I tried to do things my own way, everything went to shambles. I was learning to live completely dependent on God. Believe me when I tell you—He will take care of your every need.

One of the most unforgettable times He showed up for me was when my lights were shut off…

Let There Be Light

I received a shut-off notice from Duquesne Light stating I needed to pay $500 to restore my services. Not again, I said with frustration. I'm sick of going through this, Lord. I'm just gonna go get me a job, was my response to Jesus.

Although I knew God had done it before, I still doubted. I'd say, "The Lord will come through," but low-key I was trying to figure out how. I prayed, I believe; help my unbelief –Mark 9:24 .

I vented my frustration to an acquaintance, who suggested donating plasma and calling certain agencies. She told me about someone she knew who was in a similar predicament and had even opened a case with CYF to get her lights restored. No judgment, but I dismissed that idea with the quickness—nope, not for me.

I did, however, attempt to donate plasma. My acquaintance drove me to the center, I filled out the information, went through the interview process, only for them to tell me I couldn't donate due to low blood levels. Funny thing is, I just started smiling and talking to Jesus: "Oh, I see You…You're about to show off, aren't You?" The relationship and connection He allowed me to have with Him is unmatched. When I tell you—we did everything together. Jesus is really my boo.

On the ride back from the plasma center, I kept thinking, What are You about to do, Jesus? My acquaintance gave me more phone numbers to call. Deep down, I felt I should just call Duquesne Light, but I ignored that and dialed the other numbers. Guess what? No answer. Coincidence? I think not.

So, I finally called Duquesne Light and accidentally reached their emergency line. I told the representative my situation, unsure what to expect. All I could hear on the other end was the sound of her typing. While I waited, I just kept whispering, "Thank You, Jesus. Thank You, Jesus."

She came back on the line and said I needed $50 to restore my services. Hallelujahhh! was my response. My Godmother came to mind, so I asked her to Cash App me the money, and she did. As the rep typed again, she came back and said, "Actually, if you pay $25, we can restore your lights today."

Before I got super geeked, I asked, "What about the $500? Will I still owe it later?"

She said, "No, just the $25."

I gave her my card information immediately. My lights came back on in less than 24 hours. And God said, Let there be light –Genesis 1:3.

He showed off, and it encouraged not only me but my acquaintance too. Remember: sometimes God lets you grow through things so someone else can have a breakthrough.

I reflected on that, linking it to the Word: Let there be light. Sometimes all we have to do is speak a thing, and it happens. Not only was this a testament of His faithfulness—it was also proof of my belief that He would take care of it.

Sis, after you pray and ask Him for something, your next move should be to thank Him—not to keep on asking. He sees you, and He loves you too much to leave you in disarray.

You Are a Lender, Not a Borrower

Let me tell you what happened two months after the lights were restored. Outside of catching up on bills with the lump sum of money I received, I also paid off some delinquent accounts to improve my credit score.

My desire was to get married, but seeing my debt at over $60,000 made me feel worthless. Like, I wouldn't even marry me with all that debt. I wanted to be an asset to my future husband, not a liability—okay!

Months later, after paying off some accounts, I was listening to a Pandora interlude. I didn't catch the speaker's name, but he was talking about debt cancellation—citing Deuteronomy 15: "Every creditor shall cancel the loan he has made…"—and declaring the year of Jubilee as now. The interlude kept playing on my station, and it drew me to dig deeper.

I'd heard about some folks getting school loans forgiven, but I assumed I wouldn't qualify since I'd already graduated. Still, something nudged me to check my credit report.

To my surprise, my debt went from $60,000 to $4,000—completely gone! Yes, you read that right—$60,000, gone! Girl, when my eyes landed on that screen!?!?! Listen, I had to refresh the page to make sure I wasn't tripping. When I saw that amount again, I went crazy in the house—shouting my hallelujahs and dancing all over the place. He was making sure His princess would be an asset to His future son.

If He can do it for me, He can do it for you—maybe not in the same way, but He will show His faithfulness. He can take your little and multiply it. He's not a genie—He's a Father, a friend, He is... EVERYTHING!

Trusting God in the Waiting

Okay, so you're like, "I hear you, Yas, that He came through and turned it around in 24 hours and your debt decreased—but sis, I've been waiting for years. What do you gotta say now?"

Well... waiting is not a passive act—it is an active faith exercise. It's in the waiting that God refines us, teaching patience, endurance, and reliance on Him. Isaiah 40:31 says, "But they that wait upon the Lord shall renew their strength; they shall mount up with wings as eagles; they shall run and not be weary; and they shall walk, and not faint." The waiting season is where our strength is renewed, even when it doesn't feel like it.

Through that season, I learned:

- **God's timing is perfect.** He's always on time
- **Faith is trusting even when we can't see.** Just because we don't see movement doesn't mean God isn't working.
- **Waiting is an invitation to draw closer.** I learned to lean into Him more than ever before.

He became more than just a provider—I began to see Him as a faithful friend, a dependable Father, someone I can lean on and trust. I was learning how to do real relationship.

If you're in a waiting season right now, don't lose heart. Trust that what He has for you is worth the wait.

A moment to reflect

How do you respond when it feels like God is taking too long? Do you wait in faith, or do you try to take matters into your own hands?

Abundant Life

God doesn't just provide—He also teaches us how to steward His provision wisely. Many of us struggle not because He hasn't given us enough, but because we haven't stewarded what He has given well. We get our hands on some funds and squander them on things that don't matter. Then we find ourselves breaking down, even joking in our heads about robbing a bank just to pay the bills and feed our children. Real provision is about walking in an abundance mindset rather than a scarcity mindset.

As daughters and heirs of the Most High King, our Father has left us an inheritance in His Kingdom. We have access to His riches and glory. He has given us everything we need to live a life of Godliness, along with His very great and precious promises –2 Peter 1:3–4. As we know, the promises of God are yes and amen!

One of His promises is that He came to give us life abundantly –John 10:10. We are called to have abundance—not just financial but overflowing streams of every kind of wealth. Now, how you define wealth and how I define it might be totally different. The kind of wealth I'm speaking of is His presence, His peace, His joy, His love— the kind that makes you spin around like a little girl in a field of flowers. That's wealth. You know, the kind where all hell is breaking loose, yet your joy remains intact. The kind where, no matter what others say about you, you can still give a real smile and genuine love.

Sis, you and I have access to this kind of wealth. These are the true riches—not the ones the world chases. It may sound cliché, but I'll say it anyway: money isn't everything. Yes, it can open doors, but real wealth is a family to wake up to, a home filled with peace, the ability to love on your children, to call your parents, to check on siblings. That is the gift the world tries hard for us not to value.

Recognizing this wealth and freedom only comes from daily renewing your mind and refusing to be conformed to the world –Romans 12:2.

The Lord will open the heavens, the storehouse of His bounty, to send rain on your land in season and to bless all the work of your hands. You will lend to many nations but will borrow from none. –Deuteronomy 28:12. This reminds us that we were created to be

> Sis, you were never meant to merely strive and survive. You were created to live from faith and divine provision, not fear and financial stress.

lenders, not borrowers—to live in overflow rather than lack. But for many of us, shifting into that reality requires unlearning generational mindsets of fear and scarcity.

Sis, you were never meant to merely strive and survive. You were created to live from faith and divine provision, not fear and financial stress.

Practical Steps to Walk in Financial & Spiritual Freedom

- **Give up control:** Recognize that God—not your job, bank account, or side hustle—is your provider.
- **Practice gratitude:** Thank God in advance for what He is about to do, even before it manifests.
- **Speak life over your finances:** Proverbs 18:21 reminds us that life and death are in the power of the tongue. Declare: "I am a lender, not a borrower. God supplies all my needs."
- **Give generously:** The principle of sowing and reaping is real—when we give, God multiplies –Luke 6:38.
- **Stay in alignment:** When we remain in God's will, provision follows. Align your financial decisions with biblical principles.

Walking in financial and spiritual freedom means releasing fear, trusting God's plan, and knowing that His supply is limitless. He doesn't just want to meet your needs—He wants to bless you so you can be a blessing to others.

A moment to reflect

How do you define success and wealth?

Remember, what you desire and what God desires may be different. Be sure you're in alignment with His will for your life.

Learning to lean on the Holy Spirit wasn't easy, and it still isn't! But once you start truly letting go—whew Chile, hold onto your seatbelt—your life will never be the same. If you stop fixating on your circumstances and focus on God,

He will provide everything. You won't have to chase it; it will come to you.

MY THOUGHTS

CHAPTER ELEVEN

The Heart of the Matter

We were three months away from the It's Time to Get Up women's conference. The speakers had just met over Zoom, and everything seemed to be falling into place. I was learning, hurdling, and rejoicing all at once in preparation. But there was still one area I could not let go of—my heart.

There was this guy—let's call him Joe. I just knew he was the one I was going to marry. You could not tell me otherwise. He had everything I thought I wanted in a man: a man of God, handsome, educated, adventurous, ambitious, confident, respectful, and even practicing celibacy. Jackpot—or at least, that's what I thought. Sis, I was already thanking the Lord for sending him into my life—without even asking if this man was sent by Him. If God's design for you is to be married, then you are hand-crafted for a particular person. Like, is this your approval—or God's? Yeah, I knew that—but I didn't really know it.

My neighbor, an older wise lady, once said, "Us women see a guy we like, and before he even says hi, we're picturing ourselves down the aisle." Girl!!!!!!!!!! She didn't even know she was talking about me.

I ignored the little things that didn't sit right in my spirit—the inconsistencies, the breadcrumbing. You know just enough attention to keep me hooked. To make it worse, not once did Joe and I go to church together; heck, we didn't even pray together. But my heart wanted what it wanted. The heart is deceitful above all things and beyond cure, who can understand it. –Jeremiah 17:9. You see while I was worried about what I wanted, God knew what I needed.

Sis, we never went on a date. Sad, right? This isn't a stab at his character; it's only a revelation of what I believed I deserved. Can I tell you sis, you are precious in the Lord's sight. You are the Apple of His eye, You are fearfully and wonderfully made and you are worth more than rubies. Yes sis, God was shining His light on me and saturating me with His fountain of love as we prepared to rebuild His temple yet I still accepted the bare minimum from man. For thy maker is thine husband; the Lord of Hosts is His name; and thy redeemer the Holy one of Israel; The God of the whole earth shall he be called. –Isaiah 54:5.

If you desire marriage, then God desires that for you too. Delight yourself in the Lord and He will give you the desires of your heart; –Psalm 37:4. However, girl, enjoy your season of singleness. This is your time to grow, to seek God, and to discover who He created you to be—without distraction or compromise. Sis, you are already a wife— married to your Husbandman, the Lord your God. You are royalty, deeply loved, and fully cared for, even before any man comes along

With Joe, I was willing to accept the bare minimum. I'm embarrassed to admit this, but I've only ever been on one real date in my entire life. Every other time was a Netflix and chill kind of vibe. As long as I got a little attention it was enough for me.

That's the danger, sis—when you don't know your true worth in Christ, you'll settle for crumbs and call it a meal. I thought Joe was the one because of how we "connected." Truthfully, the first time we hung out, I really did envision us down the aisle. The crazy part? We barely even hung out. But I held onto the fantasy for two and a half years.

> When you don't know your true worth in Christ, you'll settle for crumbs and call it a meal.

Here's the part nobody talks about: you can form a soul tie without ever having sex. Soul ties come from where you invest your heart, your emotions, your dreams. Every "what if" I entertained, every moment I chose fantasy over truth, the tie got tighter. And sis, anything that ties you up outside of God's will becomes a chain. –Matthew 6:19-21.

Truth be told, Joe was the first guy I ever really took seriously. The first one I prayed for day in and day out. The first one I shared scriptures with back and forth. But here's the problem: I was the only one putting in any effort. I wanted a relationship that included God and honored Him, but a relationship takes two. I mean duh, right? I was so caught up in what I wanted that I ignored everything else.

My mentors told me he wasn't the one. My brothers, my friends, my associates all said the same thing. But I wasn't hearing any of it. You know how when you're almost done with a puzzle and there's one piece that almost fits? It's close enough that you try to force it in—because you just want it to be complete. That was me with Joe. No one could convince me otherwise.

And to be honest, part of what made it so hard was wrestling with the Word itself. I would read 1 Corinthians 13:4–7—love never gives up—and I thought that meant I had to keep holding on. I believed that continuing to pray for him was faithfulness, because the Bible says, pray without ceasing. –1 Thessalonians 5:17. To let go felt like I was giving up, and I just couldn't grasp that. However, letting go and giving up are two very different things.

Giving Up vs. Letting Go

Giving up is surrendering out of defeat—walking away before you've given your all. Letting go is different. It's surrendering in faith, trusting that after you've done your part, God will do the rest.

I had done all I could. I prayed, waited, and remained faithful. But the relationship wasn't bearing fruit. Still, I couldn't walk away. My heart wouldn't allow it. Even as we prepared for the *It's Time to Get Up* Women's Conference, I was wrestling with this weight.

One night, out of boredom, I hit Joe up. Only this time, I did something totally out of character: I asked him to send me a nude picture. Normally, Joe would've questioned me, because he knew I was reserved. But instead of pausing, he sent the picture.

The moment it came through, I felt disgusted. "Who else do you send these photos to? Eww—he's really for everybody". I thought. I texted back something along the lines of, "This is why it's hard for me. I know you deal with other women, and I just want to be the only one."

> Love that requires you to beg, chase, or prove yourself is not love at all.

Girl, don't you know he went off on me? I felt so small. But the truth? I did that to myself.

That night, I broke my own heart. And maybe that's what it took—for me to finally see the truth God and everyone else had been trying to show me. Nearly three years stuck on goofy, clinging to a fantasy. Love that requires you to beg, chase, or prove yourself is not love at all.

Two weeks later, I saw him face to face. He waved at me casually as if nothing had ever happened between us. I felt so sick. Sometimes we pray for confirmation, and God answers in ways that shake us to our core. Seeing him was not random, that was God saying, Daughter, are you done now?

I wanted to break down and cry as my chest caved in, but I held back my tears. I gave a half-smile, nodded, and turned away.

I ran to my spiritual father's office, but he wasn't there. I slammed the door shut and dropped to my knees.

And that's when I heard Holy Spirit whisper: "You know what to do."

So I got down on my knees. My legs trembled. My heart raced. I've experienced heartbreak before, I've known loss—hey, you've been reading my story—but this pain? Was by far the worst I've ever experienced at that point in my life.

I want to pause here to make note of something: the very first thing I did was run to someone else to pray for me. But they weren't there.

So, let me ask you—what will you do if your pastor or leader isn't available? You and I must learn to pray and tap into the Spirit for ourselves.

The pain of rejection was suffocating. Now only was the Lord prompting me to let go but He was making room for something greater.

Broken for Building

Two months before the It's Time to Get Up Women's Conference, God called us to fast and pray. And I cried. Every. Single. Day—literally. I didn't engage with anyone or minister to anyone. Day after day, I begged, "Take this pain away. Take away my love for this man."

Even after the whole heart attack scene, I still had mad love for Joe. But God began to clean house. November became a month of emptying—I felt stripped of everything I once held onto, it wasn't pretty. Some nights I cried so hard I could barely breathe.

Yet here's the thing about God: He doesn't just break us to leave us shattered. He breaks us to heal us right, to rebuild us stronger, and to anchor us in Him. Every tear, every moment of heartbreak, was part of His plan. To bring me back where I belonged, in Him.

Its Deeper than that

What started as heartbreak over Joe turned into something far deeper. Rejection was devastating, but it was just one layer of the cake. The more I sat with it the more God pulled back the veil—and the pain grew deeper and deeper.

It went from crying over Joe and this so-called "lost love" to reflecting on my relationship with my parents. It was like I was a tree being uprooted, roots and all and planted into Gods soil. I mean God was showing me things I have never seen before.

I began asking myself questions I had never thought to ask:

- How old were my parents when they had my siblings and me?
- What kind of childhood did they have?
- How did divorce, tragedy, and loss shape them?

And then I compared their experiences to my own. That's when I finally saw it: the patterns. Why I had a tendency to chase love. Why I did certain things.

For the first time, I could see my parents not just as Mom and Dad, but as two human beings.

That realization didn't erase the pain, but it softened my heart and opened the door for forgiveness.

Unpopular statement: Forgive your parents.

Yes, they may have dropped the ball in some areas. But they did the best they could with what they knew. Forgiving them doesn't mean disregarding your hurt. It means acknowledging the hurt, healing, and extending the same grace you want others to extend to you. Ask the Lord to remove the blinders from your eyes so you can see them the way He does.

If you can, especially if your parents are still alive, ask them questions about their upbringing. Ask the Lord to give you a heart of understanding. Forgive yourself and extend grace to yourself. What we were missing, what my parents were missing, and what we all miss as a people is love. Love is God. Keep Him at the center. Let Him bring you back to your roots, define your path, and rewrite your story.

Surrendering my heart wasn't just about letting go of Joe. It was deeper than that. It was about releasing every wound I had carried for years—the heartbreak, abandonment, rejection, the disappointments, the unresolved pain.

And that meant confronting the hardest part of all: forgiveness.

A time of Interrogation

Before we dive into forgiveness, I want to pause and share something with you. After a month of weeping, wailing, and being uprooted, I was finally able to stand on my two feet again. One morning, Pandora was playing another interlude—this time, it was Pastor Mike Jr. speaking on relationships.

I had heard it several times before, but this time it hit me differently. I knew God was speaking directly to me. So, I grabbed my pen and wrote the entire message down word for word. Here's what he said:

"It is essential, imperative, and important that we properly steward the single season. I believe you cannot steward this season right if you're looking at it the wrong way. Unfortunately, many people view singleness as a season of inconvenience. But this season is customized and created to be a season of opportunity.

An opportunity for investigation.

Sit across the table from yourself, have an interrogation session with yourself, and get to the root of who you are, and who you have been cosmically crafted, called, and created to be. Because if you engage in the act of investigation, it will lead you to a proper revelation of your value. You will always choose wrong if you don't see yourself right.

> You will always choose wrong if you don't see yourself right.

Have you ever wondered why it seems like you're picking the same person, just with a different name or body type? It's not because you're seeing them wrong; it may be because you're not seeing yourself right. You will always choose in a way consistent with what you think you deserve. Many people end up settling for less than God's best because they don't have a proper revelation—they haven't done enough investigation. Who are you? What do you want? Where are you headed? If you don't have insight and answers to these questions, you will end up suffering, chasing after someone who doesn't have a proper picture of who you've been created to be." Deep!

On December 1, 2022, I began my own interrogation. The Lord led me to Matthew 7:7, which says:

Ask, and it shall be given to you; seek, and you shall find; knock, and it shall be opened to you. For everyone who asks receives; the one who seeks finds; and to the one who knocks, it will be opened.

It was 4:45 in the morning. I sat at my table with a purple notepad and wrote down the three questions Pastor Mike Jr. had posed:

- Who are you?
- What do you want?
- Where are you headed?

Answering those questions was life changing. Writing them out gave me clarity I hadn't experienced before. For the first time, I wrote what I truly needed—not just what I wanted. If the Holy Spirit allows, I'll share my answers with you someday. This process of preparation wasn't easy, but it was necessary so I could finally rely on Him fully. Along with heartbreak and healing, true breakthrough— or rebuilding—requires one more thing: forgiveness.

MY THOUGHTS

CHAPTER TWELVE

Letting Go to Heal

For if you forgive other people when they sin against you, your heavenly Father will also forgive you. But if you do not forgive others their sins, your Father will not forgive your sins.
–Matthew 6:14–15

Forgiveness is not easy. It's a real process, especially when you've been wronged in the worst way—when the pain feels unbearable and the wound seems unforgivable. What do you do with that kind of hurt? How do you let go?

Here's the truth: holding on to anger or resentment doesn't hurt the other person—it only poisons you. Releasing it doesn't mean excusing what happened; it means choosing healing over bitterness.

> Holding on to anger or resentment doesn't hurt the other person–it only poisons you.

Out of all the places I first learned about forgiveness, it wasn't a church sermon or a book. It was from a movie.

War Room

Back in 2018, after watching the movie *War Room,* I felt inspired to create my own war room. I cleared out my closet, packed my clothes and shoes in bins, and decorated the space with scriptures on the walls to make it inviting. Every day, I would lay out a blanket, turn on the light, and read scripture. I journaled my thoughts and prayers on paper, posting them on the walls. The closet was tiny, but it didn't matter—I was determined to experience God in the same way the movie had depicted.

During this period of my life, I was learning to pray. I journaled all of my prayers—I never spoke them aloud. One night, my son erupted in anger. It was the first time I had seen him lash out this way. He was punching the walls, crying, asking, "Why did they have to take my dad? Why can't I have a dad, Mommy?" My heart broke. I hated the men who killed my son's father—not because they took him from me, but because my son was hurting, and there was nothing I could do to fix it. All I could do was listen, stay present, and be strong.

I feared my son would pick up on it. If I continued to hate those men, I worried he might act out—perhaps even worse. I was scared that he would grow up to find them and do something drastic, or that he would become a little thug because of the hatred I carried within me.

Parents, it starts with us. It's not the material things we give them; those things fade away. The best thing I could give my son was a change in behavior. He has always been my saving grace throughout my growth. If I was smoking, drinking, acting recklessly, cussing, and yelling, I would always look at him and think, "If I continue this way, I'll raise another statistic." So, I owed it to my son to be the best I could be—not just to offer him wise counsel but to embody it.

Anyway, I could no longer carry the heavy hurt in my heart for the three men who caused my family so much pain. In my war room, I wrote their names down and asked the Lord to help me forgive them, to truly let go, and to release this burden.

A few weeks later, one of the men involved in my son's father's death reached out to me on Facebook, asking for forgiveness. He expressed how sorry he was. Naturally, I immediately called one of my associates and vented. I asked if he was out of prison. She told me he wasn't—but apparently, inmates have cell phones and access to social media. I was hot! I couldn't believe he even had the luxury to reach out. All kinds of wild thoughts were running through my mind—I'm not even going to lie.

After a few days, I finally responded. I wrote, "I forgive you, but I must forgive you from a distance, and I am blocking you." God was answering that prayer—fast! And yet… it didn't feel right. Did I truly forgive him in that moment? Absolutely not. It was hard. Forgiveness isn't instant. It's not a one-and-done. It's a daily battle—a conscious choice to release the pain and step into healing.

Sometimes years can go by without a thought, and then, out of nowhere, anger or rage hits like a tidal wave. That doesn't mean you haven't forgiven them. It means the work is still ongoing. Choosing to lay it down again—and again—is what makes it real, what makes it profound.

The Mirror Exercise

Right around that time, I invested in one of Lisa Nichols' online courses, the Abundant Life Course—a 12-week program that included a focus on forgiveness. One exercise required me to take a note card and write these three things:

- Yasmin, I am proud of you for…
- Yasmin, I celebrate you for…
- Yasmin, I forgive you for…

The idea was simple but powerful: look in the mirror every day and celebrate yourself, because "what gets celebrated gets repeated." The forgiveness part was meant to heal your heart, not just check a box. I did this exercise daily, incorporating biblical principles in practical ways. It's not enough to simply ask the Lord for forgiveness; we must do our part, or we'll be waiting a lifetime! The forgiveness portion was the hardest. I would say the three men's names aloud and declare, I forgive you! I yelled, I cursed, I fought, I cried… some days, all I could do was cry—but I faced it. I continued until the tears eventually stopped. Intense? Absolutely. Worth it? Every second.

Forgiveness in Action

A few months after the man had reached out to me, I was on the bus to pick up my son from school. I wrote in my notebook, "Lord, show me where my blockage is." As soon as I got off the bus, there he was—one of the men who had contributed to the void in my son's heart and the pain in my life and my loved ones. Our eyes locked.

In that moment, I had a choice: walk toward him and cause chaos or keep moving and go get my son.

I stared at him for a moment and began walking in his direction—but then I saw my little cousin, who redirected my attention. God will make an outlet for you. It's up to you whether you'll take it or not

Free Yourself

We do not forgive for the sake of the other person; we forgive so that we can heal. We forgive so that we can move forward. We forgive so that we can lighten our hearts, which were never meant to carry such burdens alone –1 Peter 5:7. Forgiveness doesn't let the person who wronged us off the hook, but it does allow us to smile again. It's a process that takes God—it's not something we can do on our own.

> We do not forgive for the sake of the other person; we forgive so that we can heal.

I forgive to the point where I no longer harbor hate in my heart or desire revenge –Romans 12:19–21. Yet if I were to see them in public, it would still feel uncomfortable to witness them living peacefully and freely. That doesn't mean I haven't forgiven; it means my heart is still being refined. Forgiveness is a journey, not a destination, and acknowledging lingering feelings is part of the process. Healing takes time, but when we choose to release the pain, it frees us—and that is real.

> Forgiveness is a journey, not a destination

It doesn't matter who you are, where you come from, or what religion you follow. No matter what we've done, the moment we accept Jesus into our hearts as Lord and Savior, we are forgiven. As the Word of the Lord says:

If my people, who are called by my name, will humble themselves and pray, seek my face, and turn from their wicked ways, I will hear from heaven and heal their land. –2 Chronicles 7:14

Hallelujah! Jesus has already paid the price for our sins. When we turn toward Him, He offers us new life—life more abundantly.

MY THOUGHTS

CHAPTER THIRTEEN

Prepare for Landing

The Turbulence Begins

We were just one month away from reclaiming our land and stepping into His promise, but as we got closer to the finish line, the challenges grew more intense. The battle was heating up.

One of our speakers—who had been a pillar of strength and inspiration—was in the hospital with cancer. Yet even from her hospital bed, this powerful queen was still praying Heaven down, witnessing to doctors and nurses. She was leading the prayer line, waging war, and interceding while kicking cancer's butt. Her faith did not waver; she continued to show us how to stand firm even in the fire.

Her absence meant we were down a speaker—but that was nothing for God. He already knew this would happen. That's one thing we must remember in the middle of the storm: God already knows the end from the beginning.

By this time, I didn't panic. I was beginning to catch on that the Lord was already on it. So, I waited for Him to reveal who would speak at His event.

This should've been simple—until more tests came. Not only were we in need of another speaker, but we also faced yet another spiritual battle. Only this time, I wasn't the broken, fearful woman I had been before. I had learned some things along the way.

The Apple of His eye: Covered by Fire

It was almost time to pick up my son from school, but I had about 20 minutes to spare. The sun was shining, and I decided to stop by Dunkin' Donuts for a frozen coffee. I had a little extra pep in my step, smiling—it was a good day.

As I walked, I noticed a man heading in the same direction. He looked a little off, but not totally bizarre, so I paid it no mind.

When I got to Dunkin', the cashier was just about to clock out. He asked me what I wanted.

"A frozen coffee," I said.

"Okay, it's on me," he replied.

Standing in awe with a grateful heart, I said, "Forreal?! You don't gotta tell me twice… well, in that case, let me get a medium!"

I told yall "closed mouths don't get fed!"

Now, I was really in my glory. You couldn't tell me NOTHING.

But just as I was heading back toward the school, I saw the man again. He was walking behind me.

I started reciting scripture: For I, saith the Lord, will be unto her a wall of fire round about, and will be the glory in the midst of her. –Zechariah 2:5 … For he that toucheth you toucheth the apple of His eye. –Zechariah 2:8.

I walked faster. He walked faster.

I started saying the scripture out loud: "I am the apple of His eye—nobody can touch me!"

And then he started saying it out loud too.

Wait. Hold up. WHAT?!

I thought, I KNOW I am not tripping.

I slowed down just enough to listen closer, and there it was again—the same words I had just spoken, now coming from his lips. Mocking me. Mirroring me.

I told wise counsel about it later, and she said, "Yeah, girl, he was saying the truth. Nobody can touch you—you ARE the apple of His eye." I was like, "Well, when you put it that way… my God!"

As I got closer to the school building, I spotted the security guard. She saw the man trailing behind me and immediately asked, "Is he following you?"

"Yeah," I answered.

By this point, I was hyped. "Satan, I REBUKE you in the name of Jesus!"

I got all up in his face, pleading the blood of Jesus. "I'm not afraid anymore. You're gonna have to try harder than that!"

People walking by probably thought I was crazy, but I didn't care. I KNEW what was up. And I knew God was right there with me.

The security guard stepped in and asked the man, "Is there a problem? Are you following her?"

The man shook his head. "No." Then he walked away. Just like that.

Some of the same staff who had helped last time with the "straggler man" were there again, standing in disbelief. They were probably thinking, what kind of life is this lady living? But listen—they didn't see what I saw, nor did they know what I knew.

My son finally came out of the building, and we headed toward the bus stop.

At first, I didn't tell him what had just happened. Even though I had been bold and courageous in the moment, I was lowkey shook.

But let me tell you how awesome my God is.

As my son and I walked toward the bus stop, I ran into my mother. Y'all—my MOM!

I jumped on her with the quickness and hugged her so tight, like my life depended on it. Tears welled in my eyes as I clung to her.

"God sent you," I said, catching my breath. "He knew I needed a mother's hug."

I could've broken right then and there, but I didn't need to. God was holding me up. Through my mom, He was saying, I see you, daughter. I'm right here.

And just like that, He reminded me that everything was alright. I could relax.

Sis, I'm telling you—God will give you what you need, right when you need it.

Pressure before Promise

Even after standing boldly in my faith and rebuking the enemy face-to-face, the challenges didn't stop coming. If anything, they increased. It was as if every force was trying to break me right before the promise. And on top of that, more unexpected obstacles kept piling up.

> The closer you get to the promise the more relentless the battle becomes.

The closer you get to the promise the more relentless the battle becomes. This was intentional; the enemy knew that my next step would break chains for generations. But this time, I was ready for war. The enemy wanted to shake me, but I was planted.

Im not going to blame everything on the enemy. God puts us through these tests too—to build our character.

It was wild. Some of the children who were supposed to participate in the conference quit the dance selection. Even though we were blessed with a worship leader, we didn't have anyone to handle the music. A million tiny details were falling by the wayside, which felt overwhelming and discouraging—especially with less than a month to go before the rebuilding of His temple.

I felt the weight of every expectation, every detail, every unanswered question. It wasn't just about an event—it was about souls being healed, about releasing God's glory to His people who so desperately needed Him. The worship leader, the hostess, everyone involved expected answers, but I couldn't provide any because I had to wait on Him. The pressure was on! I sat and pondered, "Could I handle the vision God placed inside me?"

While scrolling through Facebook, I came across a post from one of the speakers for the It's Time to Get Up Women's Conference. He wrote:

"As you move towards your purpose, the challenges you face become more difficult. The rain falls harder, the floods rise quicker, and the winds blow more fiercely. But just like a flight attendant advises passengers to prepare for landing...#PrepareForLanding

#HoldOnJustALittleWhileLonger.

Those words hit me deep. When the going gets tough, we, too, must brace ourselves and hold on just a little while longer. I needed a miracle, and I needed one fast!

Divine Alignment

> God places people in our path to help carry the vision.

The Lord provided everything we needed—just in time. Our worship leader connected us with someone who could direct the music for the conference. Just like that—a critical need was met. I was learning the power of divine alignment. God places people in our path to help carry the vision. This lesson appears throughout this book, but imma say it till I cant say it no more. I had to learn to trust—not just in God's provision—but in the people He was sending, because they were part of His provision. Often, the people we are linked to carry the very things we lack.

That's why it's so important to walk through life with others. But hear me, sis—not everybody you're around is meant to walk with you. You must be certain that the people you connect with are sent by Him. There is an anointing on your life that some people cannot handle. You are not meant for everybody, and everybody is not meant for you. As a daughter of the King, you cannot afford to just hang out with anyone. Stop befriending everyone. Use discernment. Ask Him for revelation about whom you are meant to connect with.

As the African proverb says, "If you want to go fast, go alone; if you want to go far, go together." Even now—this is still something I am learning.

The blessings of the Lord continued to roll in. As I scrolled through Facebook again, I came across a post about a prayer line. Even though it was the last week of December, the post reminded me that God is still in the business of working miracles. I took it as a sign. Without hesitation, I dialed in, expecting Him to show up. Faith is believing without seeing. –Hebrews 11:1

With joy, I greeted the prayer line's hostess as I joined the call. She welcomed me warmly, and after the service, asked me to stay on the line so we could exchange numbers. She sensed a divine connection between us—though at the time, neither of us fully understood what God was setting in motion.

A few days later, I couldn't stop thinking about her. There was a strong prompting in my spirit to invite her to speak at the It's Time to Get Up Women's Conference. I had no idea about the depth of her work—but I knew God was saying, this is the one.

Despite my hesitation, I picked up the phone and called her. Without a doubt, she immediately agreed to speak.

And let me tell you—this woman was a force! An absolute powerhouse. A woman after God's heart, and a true ambassador for Christ. Thats what happens when we obey to the Lord and submit to His will. We get to see Him work in every detail.

But here's where it gets even crazier…

A few days later, I discovered that the man who had agreed to direct the music for the conference was actually her nephew!

Listen… God is divine. He is intentional. He is the Master Orchestrator.

I stood in awe of how He was aligning everything—every piece, every person, every detail—coming together at the exact time and place it was supposed to.

Teachability: A Lesson Across Generations

During the course of this journey, God provided me with one woman I confided in about everything. We all need that one person with whom we can be completely honest and not have to pretend that everything is okay when it's not. People are indeed a gift, and we should treat them as such, because the Lord doesn't have to allow us to have anyone.

I met this woman during my leadership course in the technology class. Our relationship is a true example of "Bridging the Gap" between generations, as she is much older than me. Yet despite the age difference, that's my girl. We respect each other and learn from one another, which is truly an honor and a privilege.

The seasoned women need the younger women, and the younger women need the seasoned women—period. We must be open to receiving one another. Younger women must recognize that we don't know everything, and seasoned women must also understand that they can learn from the younger generation. At the end of the day, we all must remain teachable.

We need each other to survive.

A Brief Message to You

Attention older women: We value and appreciate your presence in our lives. However, please stop judging us. It is true that we do not have the knowledge and experiences you've had, but just because we are young does not mean we haven't experienced some things. We need your wisdom—and believe it or not, we truly want to glean from it. You are still needed, just as Titus 2 reminds us.

Attention younger women: Please listen attentively and keep an open heart to the wisdom of your elders. The truth sis, we don't know everything. It's only right to acknowledge that the prayers of our grandmothers—and those who came before us—have paved the way for where we stand today.

Furthermore, we must learn to be patient with one another and appreciate one another. Only then can we truly bridge the gap between generations. –1 Corinthians 12:15–26

During one of our conversations, my friend gave me some valuable advice. She told me not to give up because people were waiting for me on the other side. She also advised me to shift my focus from the storm and instead focus on God. (Wheew, that's a whole sermon by itself!) When we focus on the storm, it becomes all we can see. But when we focus on God, hope arises, and we can face any challenge with faith. The impossible becomes possible.

When we begin to believe in something far beyond ourselves, that's when real change takes place. It was in this space of faith and surrender that I witnessed God's divine orchestration yet again.

We Made It: But the Finish Line Ain't the End

On January 14, 2023, the *It's Time to Get Up Women's Conference* finally happened! After rejection, weeping, and uprooting, it was time to step into destiny. I had attended plenty of women's conferences before, but this one—I had the privilege and honor to help organize. I dusted off my dream, took it off the shelf, and ran with it. This wasn't about me; it was an assignment only God could get the glory for.

The conference was indescribable. God's presence filled the room in ways words can't capture. Laughter, joy, connections, unity—it overflowed. Healing happened. Strongholds broke. Breakthroughs were birthed. I stood at the front, looking at women—some in tears, some worshipping, some sitting still, soaking it all in. It was happening. Every battle, every setback, every moment of doubt suddenly made sense. Freedom saturated the room—chains fell, hearts opened, spirits soared. It was pure, it was real, it was holy.

Yes, I faced challenges. But I persevered with God. I fought fears, braved storms, endured being misunderstood. Still, I kept going, trusting Him with all my heart. He carried me through every obstacle, and now I walk freely. The cycle is broken. A new story begins for generations to come. God took my pain and turned it into purpose.

I thought it was over. I thought there was no hope. But God heard my cry. He washed away guilt and shame, healed my wounds, and restored my joy. I had to die so I could live! Know this: there is purpose in your pain. Every trial, tear, and setback—it's all working for your good –Romans 8:28. The visions and dreams God planted in your heart were not accidental. He trusts you because He knows what He put inside of you. –Ephesians 2:10 And when the time is right, you will step into it.

Question for you: what happens when you step into the promise, and it still doesn't look like what you expected? What do you do when you climb the mountain, cross the finish line, and instead of celebration, you're met with silence—or yet another waiting season?

MY THOUGHTS

CHAPTER FOURTEEN

I Have Decided

When Fulfillment Seems Far

A few weeks after the It's Time to Get Up Women's Conference, I found myself on the phone with wise counsel, pouring out my frustration.

I felt empty.

I had planned to launch an online coaching course. One moment, I was promoting it with full confidence, and the next, I had to cancel because the funds just weren't there. I was super annoyed—I thought that after the conference, I'd have the resources to keep creating.

What did I do with the earnings from the conference, you ask?

First off, it wasn't much. Still, it was pretty cool to put something together and actually get paid for it—epic, right? I chose to bless those who had poured their time, energy, and hearts into rebuilding the temple. I couldn't pay them, but I bought small gifts as a way of honoring their service.

In my mind, once the conference was over, doors would open— more gatherings, book publishing, merchandise sales, maybe even my own building for my girls' group. Your girl had plans! –Proverbs 19:21

But then my sister hit me with a hard truth:

"You want to make God laugh? Tell Him your plans."

Ouch. Just slap me, why don't ya!

Even after witnessing God move in miraculous ways, I still wasn't satisfied. Isn't that our default response? "Lord, I know You did this for me, but I want more."

So, I asked, What am I supposed to do with my life now, Lord? The silence shook me. Lord, You know I need to know the next move, lol. I thought I had finally arrived. But Chile, the only time you truly arrive is when it's your time to go to heaven—and we better pray that's where we end up.

As I vented to wise counsel, she said:

"Oh girl, don't you worry about anything. You never know what God has for you. The very thing you need may be the thing someone else already has. You just stay open!"

Without Borders

One day, I volunteered at The Connect Center in East Pittsburgh—an outreach ministry led by one of the speakers from the conference.

They were hosting Teen Night, which was right up my alley. So, I volunteered.

When I walked in, I was completely amazed.

This place. The vision. The goals. The mission. It matched mine in ways I couldn't ignore.

Even down to the color of the walls.

I stood there, in awe.

One room was the exact same color as the one we used for my girls' group, Embracing All of Me—Not only that—it was the same color as my for-profit organization, Striving for His Excellence!

God. Was. Up. To. Something.

I had written the vision YEARS ago.

And here I was—walking into it.

For years, I had questioned if I heard God right. Had I been chasing a dream that was never going to happen? But standing there, surrounded by the thing I'd envisioned, I knew—this was no coincidence. This was divine alignment. The colors, the mission, the purpose—it was like God had been prepping this place just for me all along. I had been stressing over the "how," but He had already handled the "when."

A few weeks later, I had an intense prayer session—not for myself, but for the owner of The Connect Center. A powerful prayer session indeed.

I got off my knees, checked my email, and there it was. A message from the owner that read something like this:

"It's time to walk in your calling. The time is now. If you're ready to make an impact, meet us at The Connect Center on [date]."

This email wasn't just for me—it went out to others as well.

I had no clue what was coming next.

But I knew one thing for sure: This was the next step I had been seeking God for!

Holy Ground

On March 5, 2023, I found myself stepping into something I never saw coming helping plant a church.

"Lord… what?! A church?!"

As my relationship with Jesus deepened, I often asked Him the same thing David did:

"Can I just dwell in Your house forever?" –Psalm 27:4

Well, He answered.

LITERALLY.

This was church like no other—not bound by tradition, not filled with routine, but overflowing with the raw, undeniable presence of the Holy Spirit.

I had a choice to make.

I was now serving at two churches—my home church, Liberty Baptist, and this new ministry at The Connect Center.

At the same time, my old job reached out, offering me my former position—with DOUBLE the pay.

Tempting. It would've helped fund my coaching course, secure my next steps, and bring stability.

But something felt off.

God had been providing for me every step of the way—so why did going back feel like moving backward?

I asked God for a clear sign.

And He gave it.

The next day, I was walking my son to baseball practice when I spotted a $20 bill on the ground.

Right then, I knew taking my old position back wasn't the move.

I canceled my meeting with my old supervisor.

And guess what happened?

My phone got disconnected, my gas bill was due, and I didn't have the money.

Notice the pattern? The enemy was trying to hit me with darts, hoping I'd panic. Logic said, "Go back to the job. Secure the bag."

But my spirit wouldn't let me. God had brought me this far—would I really turn back now? –Hebrews 10:38-39 What if this was another test, I thought.

Miracles come in all sizes, shapes, and forms. There are millions—trillions—happening every day. Sometimes the biggest ones are ordinary: waking up, seeing the sun, having a place to pray. My beautiful sis do not just look for God in the giant moments—see Him in the quiet, in the seemingly ordinary. That man is always blessing!

I had to decide. Listen, that trust piece is a wild boy. Yes, I still struggle with it, even after everything He's done.

So of course, I'm freaking out:

"Lord, did I make the wrong choice?"

That afternoon, I jumped on the prayer line with my new church. I was so blue I didn't want to speak.

> True faith is resting in the hands of the Father, knowing He will supply all your needs.

"Lord, please do not let them call on me to pray."

Of course—they called me to lead prayer. As soon as I opened my mouth, I wailed. I let it all out. Guess what their response was? They listened, gave me space to break, filled me up spiritually, and took care of my bills.

God gave me community again. He gave me provision again. He gave me a space to be vulnerable—and He showed up. This is what happens when we are adopted into His family.

True faith is resting in the hands of the Father, knowing He will supply all your needs. A life truly dependent on the Father I lived. –Philippians 4:19

MY THOUGHTS

CHAPTER FIFTEEN

Are You Willing to Be Sent?

Purification

Earlier, I talked about Esther's courage to fast for her people. But before her bold stand came a season of preparation—a time of purification that positioned her for purpose. I recall her courage and willingness to follow God for her people's sake. She was an ordinary girl—just like us—whose "yes" opened a door she never imagined. Fascinatingly, the book of Esther never mentions God's name, yet His presence is all over it.

The Bible doesn't detail Esther's upbringing or wealth, but we know she lost her parents and was raised by her uncle or cousin, depending on the translation. She was a Jewish orphan, yet God called her to become Queen, living out her royal birthright!

Royalty doesn't just mean fancy dresses or people waiting on you. Royalty is servanthood—knowing who you are and whose you are. It's unlearning old ways and becoming who God created you to be. Royalty is a calling, a purpose. **Royalty is… you.**

> Royalty is servanthood

God searches for someone willing to say "Yes." In Isaiah 6:8, He asked, "Whom shall I send?" Isaiah answered, "Here am I; send me." Are you ready to surrender your understanding and step into the unique purpose He formed for you? Will you be brave enough to let go of your need to control "why" and trust His plan? It won't be easy, but it's worth it. Your "yes" doesn't just free you—it frees those connected to you.

Before Esther could own her destiny, she and other women spent a year in purification—six months with oil and myrrh, then six with perfumes and cosmetics –Esther 2:12. This process was necessary before she could walk through God's predestined door. In "Greater is Coming," Jekalyn Carr mentions how the olive must endure shaking, beating, and pressing for the oil to flow. I felt like Esther, facing my own shaking, beating, and pressing as I prepared to deliver God's baby—His temple, the "It's Time to Get Up" Conference.

I have an opinion (not stated in the Bible) that Esther's beauty treatments weren't just for outward appeal; they also rebuilt her character. It was the same for me—shaking, beating, and pressing. It wasn't just about organizing a conference; it was about laying down my life for the King, doing what He created me to do—becoming partners with God.

Just like you, too, have gone through shaking, beating, and pressing. God is looking for a bride without blemish. A church without spot.

Discipleship as Purification

One thing I've learned over the years is that, as a church, we often fail when it comes to discipling one another. We celebrate when someone gives their life to Christ, but what happens next? Where is the follow-up?

I remember when I received Jesus as my Lord and Savior. The church was excited, welcoming me into the Kingdom, and I was filled with joy. I took about three classes on baptism. After completing those classes, I was baptized.

But that was it.

As a newborn babe in Christ, I was left to figure things out on my own. There were no mature brothers or sisters walking alongside me, guiding me through the next steps in my spiritual journey. No one discipled me. And because of that, I found myself in a vulnerable position.

Shortly after my baptism, different religious groups started reaching out to me, trying to recruit me into their beliefs. They were evangelizing, and the scariest part? Many of these religions seemed eerily similar to Christianity. If I hadn't sought God for myself, I could have easily been led in the wrong direction.

This is where I believe we fail as the body of Christ. Salvation is just the beginning. The real work comes in the journey that follows. As daughters of the Most High, it is our duty to walk alongside new believers—to disciple them, to equip them, to strengthen them in their faith. It's not just about salvation; it's about relationship. It's about helping one another grow in Christ, not just introducing people to Him and leaving them to figure it out alone.

Discipleship is itself a purification process. It shapes us, humbles us, and prepares us for greater.

I experienced this first-hand. In one discipleship class that lasted several months, we studied Scripture deeply and applied it to real life. One day, our instructor invited us for dinner and washed our feet, like Jesus in John 13:2–17. It was humbling and unforgettable. Another time, my mother-in-love, Charece, told me about a technology course at a seminary. Though I wasn't tech-savvy, she encouraged me to go, and I said yes. I didn't just learn skills—I learned teamwork, accountability, and how to love people even in tough conversations. God was teaching me how to walk with others, even as He purified me.

Through those experiences, God cleansed me of my sins, stretched me in new ways, and taught me how to sit at His feet. Discipleship was part of my purification—it wasn't only about me being poured into, but also about learning to pour out.

Esther wasn't the only woman called to walk into this destiny, but as Scripture says, many are called, but few are chosen. –Matthew 22:14 She diligently sought God's guidance, trusted Him and obeyed, and stayed faithful while learning to fight her battles with Him by her side. As a result of her faithfulness, God chose Esther, restoring her to the woman He intended her to be.

There's an Esther in each of us. Many face life's trials but haven't reached their fullest potential because they haven't fully surrendered to Christ. Only by denying ourselves daily do we walk in our destined fullness.

Maybe you think you're just teaching the students now, but you can't see how many families you are impacting. Maybe you assume owning a store is just business, but imagine the community change it could spark. Our lives are really designed for others. We can not take any of this stuff when we are called home. Instead, we have a purpose on this earth: to shine, so others recognize their own light. That recognition leads to freedom—true freedom in Christ, our Lord and Savior.

When you trust Him, you might not know what, when, or how, but if you answer His call, He'll supply every need. You may feel inadequate—lacking resources, connections—but as a living witness, I say none of that matters. What matters is your "Yes."

The process is necessary. To receive God's best, we need certain qualities and fruit –Galatians 5:22–23. We must be purified because God won't compromise with our hearts, motives, or attitudes—He wants them pure and Christlike.

God's provision isn't just about what He gives—it's about who we become in the process. Like Esther, we must be willing to go through purification, knowing that what awaits us is worth the refining.

MY THOUGHTS

CHAPTER SIXTEEN

Fully Known and Loved by Him

Remember at the beginning of this book when I told you my car was repossessed? That happened right when I hit the ground running, starting to build for the It's Time to Get Up Conference. One of my desires during that season was to have a vehicle again.

Not long after, my new pastor at The Connect Center, Connected Community Ministries recommended a four-week car-buying workshop that was hosted by Divine Restoration Church. By the end of it, those who attended every class would receive a down payment toward a vehicle. The blessing was set to be announced during Divine Restorations 10-year anniversary celebration—just one week after my birthday, June 2, 2023.

When they called the three participants forward to receive their blessing, the Lord did what He always does—exceedingly, abundantly more –Ephesians 3:20.

My pastor spoke kindly of me, thanking me for the work I had contributed to the ministry. Then, the entire congregation sang

Happy Birthday to me. To top it off, they handed me a beautiful bouquet of flowers.

It was the greatest gift I had ever received. So much love, so much joy. For the first time ever, I was completely mute. That kind of love could only come from God.

Both my new church, Connected Community, and Divine Restoration gifted my son and me a vehicle—paid in full. Let me tell you something, sis: you are fully known and loved by God. It wasn't about the vehicle, but about the love and appreciation I had genuinely never received in a natural sense before.

There were three of us who completed the workshop series. Two of us were gifted with a vehicle, and one was gifted a down payment toward a vehicle. All of this happened on a Sunday.

The Calm Before the Storm

To retrieve my keys, I needed insurance coverage. On Monday, I got coverage and was able to take our vehicle off the lot. With everything that had happened, a sense of calmness overwhelmed me.

One would think that someone experiencing this level of love and joy would be telling the world. Yet, I did not. Honestly, I was still in awe. I didn't go out to get car accessories or call my people to share the good news.

The Unexpected Turn

I was talking to my mom in love on Wednesday afternoon, and she asked why I sounded so sad. She said, "Girl, you should be shouting with joy right now."

I assured her I was happy—just tired. I didn't want to go to sleep, so I took the car out for a drive to the park to read my Bible and work on my manuscript.

As I sat in the park, glorifying God and thanking Him for all His goodness, I basked in the sun and just dwelled with Him. I did write a little, but not as much as I thought I would. I got thirsty and decided to stop at the store and then head back home. Before I got back into the vehicle, I said:

Trust in the Lord with all your heart. Lean not unto your own understanding, but in all your ways acknowledge Him, and He will direct your path. –Proverbs 3:5

I repeated the scripture three times, then asked the Lord what He was trying to tell me.

After sitting there for a little while, I said, "Okay, Lord, I am trusting You." I got in the car and headed toward the store. My music was not loud, and the roads were clear on all sides.

Next thing you know—**CRASHHHHH!!!!** Head-on collision.

One moment, I was praising God for His awesomeness. Next, I was staring at airbags and shattered glass. The ambulance and people came to the car, asking, *"Are you okay?"*

While I gathered my bearings, I quickly went to the other car to ensure they were okay. It happened so fast… almost as if the van was placed there. Thankfully, no one got hurt. I walked away from a deadly accident. Airbags erupted, and everything.

His Presents or His Presence

The next day, I was sitting in a meeting with my pastor, planning for our next worship service. The following weekend, I ministered in song at my home church, Liberty Baptist, for the last time. The song was titled I'm Gonna Be Ready by Yolanda Adams.

The accident left me with so many questions, but it also deepened my faith. I didn't understand why God would allow that to happen. It was also extremely embarrassing. I thought, "Lord, why bless me in front of everyone only to take it away?"

> I was being sanctified–made pure, holy, tried, and true. He needed to see if I was after His presents or His presence.

It was never about the car—it was the Lord's way of saying: I see you. I love you. You are mine.

Just as the Lord used Job for His glory, He was also using me. The Lord giveth, and the Lord taketh away. -Job 1:21 I was being sanctified—made pure, holy, tried, and true. He needed to see if I was after His presents or His presence.

Many times, we get caught up in receiving His promises. But the things He promises—the glimpses of success that He reveals—are only to encourage us as we learn to walk with Him. Ultimately, Jesus is the Miracle. He is the Promise. And if I'm honest, I often lose sight of that.

> To be loved, to be seen, to be forgiven, to be whole, to be chosen, to be redeemed, to have peace, to be healed, to experience true divine relationship– these are the true treasures in life, found only in Him.

We must recognize that we were solely made for the Master— not for our own gain, but for the glory of God.

To be loved, to be seen, to be forgiven, to be whole, to be chosen, to be redeemed, to have peace, to be healed, to experience true divine relationship—these are the true treasures in life, found only in Him.

He promises us a land flowing with milk and honey. The milk represents the basic foods we need as believers—such as His Word, and prayer. The honey represents the gift of Him. His presence is the gift. Everything else is extra.

Your dreams, ambitions, desires—they are nothing compared to getting to know Him. The One who loved us enough to die for us. The One who created you and me.

> Your dreams, ambitions, desires—they are nothing compared to getting to know Him.

Always Learning

No matter how much we grow in the Lord, we are always learning at new levels. Even when we think we know something, I've learned that I don't know a darn thing. Each season is new, and every day is different. How He decides to use you or provide for you yesterday may not be the way He shows up the next.

What is He calling you to?

Whatever it is, don't hesitate. Give Him your full *"YES"* today. He's been waiting for it.

If you would've told me back then—when I was struggling, questioning, and waiting—that I'd be standing here today, fully walking with God…I wouldn't have believed you. If you'd said this is how my life would turn out, I'd have called you a fool.

But God.

He always knew. I wouldn't trade it for the world. The best part? This is just the beginning. And He knows what He's doing with you too.

Being confident of this, that He who began a good work in you will carry it on to completion until the day of Christ. –Philippians 1:6

Step boldly, beloved—your season of faith, purpose, and victory is here.

This time, I am living for Him!

MY THOUGHTS

Final Message

Thank you, sis, for walking through my journey with me, and I'm excited to walk alongside yours too. Because I know you know—it's your time, right?

You are loved. You are needed. For such a time as this.

I'm telling you, sis—you've tried it your way so many times, in so many ways. Now try Jesus. For real this time. He won't fail. Oh, I won't say it will be a life of ease and no pain but baby, you will be protected, covered, loved, and taken care of like never before. You will have everlasting joy that no one can take away.

You already have everything inside of you.

It's time to look within.

A Prayer for You

Father God, in the name of Jesus, I thank You for this woman of God. Bless her and keep her, Lord. Give her a fresh revelation of who You are. Breathe on her, Lord, and resurrect those dry bones. The dreams and visions she thought were dead—may they come alive even now, in the name of Jesus.

Thank You, Lord, for her relationship with You. May she experience Your love in a way she has never known before. Father, You have called her by name and set her apart—for she is chosen and created to do good works that You prepared for her before she was even formed in her mother's womb.

We cancel every lie of the enemy that tells her she's not good enough. We rebuke the adversary and send him back to the pit of hell where he came from! Every chain that has tried to hold her down—be broken NOW, in Jesus' name!

May everything connected to her be blessed and protected. She is the curse breaker in her family. She will be a light and a testimony to the very people You have called her to.

Shape her. Make her. Mold her into the woman You have destined her to be. No weapon formed against her shall prosper. Every tongue that rises against her shall be silenced.

Father, we thank You for favor over her life. We thank You for divine connections, divine opportunities, and divine wisdom. Lord, surround her with the right people at the right time. Let her walk in boldness and confidence, knowing that You have gone before her and made the crooked paths straight.

She is blessed in the city. She is blessed in the field. She is blessed in her coming in and her going out.

Lord, let Your will be done in her life. May her family witness the goodness of God through her, and may many come to Christ because of her testimony.

Lord, keep her humble. Give her divine wisdom and strategy to carry out every assignment You've placed in her hands. May kindness be on her lips, wisdom be in her tongue, and Your favor follow her everywhere she goes.

Her children will rise up and call her blessed. Her husband also. For beauty is vain, but a woman who fears the Lord shall be praised.

Thank You, Lord, for giving her a heart like Yours. Create in her a clean heart and renew a right spirit within her.

She will walk in the fruit of the Spirit—love, peace, joy, gentleness, patience, and long-suffering.

Lord, we thank You that she lacks nothing. She has everything she needs, and most importantly, she will always recognize Your covenant with her.

You love her for eternity.

We seal this prayer in the blood of Jesus.

In Jesus' name, Amen.

Now go and walk in your calling

Becoming

Most people will see the grave before ever discovering who they are. "Everybody dies, but not everybody lives."

I always knew I had a purpose. I didn't know exactly what it was, but I knew there was something significant I was meant to do—humbly speaking! Ever since I attended the 2021 Women Evolve Conference, one of my favorite scriptures has been Jeremiah 1:5.

Before I formed you in the womb I knew you, before you were born I set you apart; I appointed you as a prophet to the nations. –Jeremiah 1:5

The way Pastor Sarah Jakes broke that thang down was phenomenal. After she broke it down, she left us with something to ponder:

"Lord, bring me back to the original intent of my being."

Sis… I haven't been the same since.

I wasn't just placed on assignment in that season—in the preparation, I was discovering myself. I meditated on that scripture, and I don't mean sitting cross-legged or chanting. Initially, I thought that's what it meant. But I learned that to meditate means to sit with it, study it, define the words that stand out, and let them roll in your mind all day—the same way we rehearse our grocery lists or replay conversations. That's what we ought to do with the Word of God.

The more I studied, the more I began to truly see me. One day I was staring in the mirror, amazed at my reflection. I smiled and said, "Wow, look at me, Daddy—You look good!" I couldn't stop touching my face. My face was so radiant. At first I tried wiping my face thinking maybe it was just oily. But the shine was still there. So I used a washcloth yet the beauty didn't fade. It was me natural as can be.

To add to that sacred moment, I received a text from Lady Janelle—because that's just like God, sending something so timely. It was a performance by Cynthia Erivo titled I Am Here. During that performance, one of the songs she sang was Mona Lisa by Jazmine Sullivan. These lyrics captured exactly what I was feeling:

"My eyes ain't used to these rays, I'm feeling exposed, but I hide no more… As the sun shines on all of my glory, my flaws don't look so bad at all…Every part of me is a vision of a portrait of Mona, of Mona Lisa. Every part of me is beautiful and I finally see I'm a work of art, a masterpiece."

Girl, when you have a moment, look it up—it will bless your whole entire spirit.

To be honest, I never saw myself as beautiful. I had a nice build, but I always believed that was the only reason guys noticed me. I never left the house without lashes because I didn't feel fabulous without them. But during that wilderness season, I was determined to discover the real me. I chopped my hair—I always wore it short and relaxed, but this time, I wanted to grow it back naturally, to see *all* of me, the real me. I was determined for God to bring me back to the original intent of my being.

I grew confident and bold. I was radiant, sure of where I was headed, and clothed in strength and dignity. I laughed without fear of the future –Proverbs 31:25. I was able to experience this because I stayed submitted, committed and focused on Him.

Every morning, I would wake up and worship, pray, read my Word, journal, write affirmations, and map out my day—giving all of it to God. Then I would go for a walk, clean the house, make sure dinner was ready, and pack my son's lunch—all of this was done before it was time to wake him up for school in the morning. I was walking proverbs 31 out all crazy. I had energy to plan for the conference, pray with someone in need, and tackle things that came up. I set clear boundaries. I didn't answer my phone or take calls without consulting God first. I was laser focused.

My family had meetings about me, wondering if I had lost my mind (lol). They didn't see this as "work" because it didn't earn a paycheck. But baby, I was getting paid. My house was in order. My environment was peaceful. Every time I left the house I'd shout, "Good morning, world!" when I stepped outside, thanking God for the fresh air, the chirping birds, and the blooming flowers. I was so in love with Jesus—alive even in what seemed like my darkest hour. I found the missing key to life: Him. Nothing could get in the way of my relationship with Him—nothing. I'm telling you, sis—that level of love isn't something He's just given to me. Nah, it's yours too.

The scripture weeping may endure for the night but joy comes in the morning Psalm 30:5 doesn't just mean the next day.

There is joy in the morning and in the mourning. He gave me beauty for my ashes and sunshine for the rain.

It's also talking about in the mourning. All the depression, sadness, and grief were lifted—no more. There is joy in the morning and in the mourning. He gave me beauty for my ashes and sunshine for the rain.

Even when I felt lonely or longed for romance, I'd go on dates with God. I'd dress up, twirl, and dance. He would paint the sky so beautifully. In those moments, I realized something: Jesus likes to have fun too. We didn't just sit in solemn worship or only listen to gospel music; we laughed, played, and chilled together. Sometimes I'd get carried away, and He would lovingly reel me back in. But oh, the joy of it all! That song "Falling in Love with Jesus" by Kirk Whalum—was so real to me.

Make no mistake its not always lollipops and rainbows, sis. Trials still come, desires still rise, but you are never alone. He understands everything—your cravings, your questions, your heart, your whole self. And in that, you find freedom to be fully you, right there in His presence. Intentional in every step. Maybe you've forgotten how free you are, but rest assure; you are. Return to your Creator—your Maker, your Husbandman, your Father. Let Him remove all the trash piled on your treasure. Let Him bind your wounds, heal you, and breathe life into you again. Learning to just be instead of doing.

Scriptures I Leaned On specifically in my intimate relationship with Him

- Psalm 91:1–2: Literally lived in His presence
- Proverbs 31: The woman of valor was so inspiring I mean who doesn't want to be like her
- Isaiah 54:5: He is my Maker, Husband, and Redeemer.

And every scripture that spoke on submission. I literally conducted my relationship with Christ as my husbandman.

I dove into the Bible like it was Google. My King James concordance, gifted by my then-pastor from Liberty Baptist—honestly, the best gift I've ever received besides the people God placed in my life—became my constant companion. That Bible wasn't just a book; it became my best friend. I would open it and search topics like submit, love, gift, etc. and at the back of the book you'd find related scriptures on that specific topic. Which was a great study tool.

From those seasons of discipline, worship, and surrender, I discovered 20 traits that a woman of God grows into as she becomes all that He created her to be. Please note that becoming is constant and the woman He calls you to be in one season may not be the same in the next.

20 Traits A woman who is becoming possess

1. She makes wise investments.
2. She recognizes her body as a temple.
3. She doesn't mind being alone.
4. She chooses peace over chaos.
5. She knows her value.
6. She keeps from gossiping.
7. She's sober-minded.
8. She's clean.
9. She worries less.
10. She dresses like royalty.
11. She is productive.
12. She plans and organizes.

13. She's about what she talks about.
14. She's not easily offended.
15. She takes time for herself.
16. She embraces the beauty around her.
17. She's teachable.
18. She examines her heart.
19. She's humble.
20. She cultivates a relationship with God.

What kind of woman do you want to be?

- Write it down.
- Then become her.
- What makes you feel alive?
- What legacy will you leave?
- What is your purpose?
- What are you passionate about?

Take a moment to sit with these questions. Let God speak as you write.

Confession & Reflection

I needed this reminder. Even while living for Him, I sometimes placed everything else first—the ministry, the people, the schedule. And when I did that, I lost myself.

This life with Him is not a joke. It's not religion; it's relationship. Just like in a marriage—or any other meaningful relationship—you have to work at it every day: in the good, the bad, the ugly, and everything in between. Not just when you feel like it.

Question

When was the last time you truly spent time with Him?

Becoming is a journey. I am not who I was when He first called me. I am not the same woman I was when I wrote this book. My skills have grown, my abilities have expanded, but if I do not sit with Him—if we do not return to Him—the people He wants to reach will remain bound. We are always evolving. As we evolve, our relationship with God must evolve too.

For those who are just beginning their walk with Jesus—enjoy it to the fullest. Stay focused. And as Lady Janelle would say, "Bloom where you are planted."

Here are a few scriptures to glean from in this season of growth

Matthew 6:33, Psalm 37:4, Psalm 91:1–3, Ephesians 1–2, Jeremiah 29:11–14, Jeremiah 33:3, John 10:10, Galatians 2:20, Galatians 5:22.

Prayer for Purpose

Heavenly Father, as my sister seeks You for purpose, thank You for revealing Yourself to her in ways only she can understand. Lord, thank You for undistracted devotion. Heal her from the wounds of her past—from childhood until now—and replace that pain with Your love, in Jesus' name.

May she find comfort in You alone. Help her to see herself the way You do—fearfully and wonderfully made. Thank You for the calling on her life and for giving her the confidence to step forward into what

You have planned. Bless her family and her children. Cover her with Your divine protection and surround her with Your presence

Lord, may she know who she is and whose she is. Bless her from the crown of her head to the soles of her feet. Send divine helpers, meet every need, and let her cup overflow. Every lying tongue that rises against her, cancel it now in the name of Jesus. Forgive her for any words spoken over herself that did not align with Your truth. Every attack sent to destroy her, we send back to the pit of hell. We love You, Lord, and thank You for her life. Keep her and cover her in Jesus' name. Amen.

Prayer for Renewal

For those who feel it's been a while since you've been intimate with Jesus—those who are doing the work of the Lord but are worn out and tired—do not beat yourself up. Give yourself grace. Take a step back and allow Him to pour new wine into you. Return to Him and lay down your old flames.

Neither height nor depth, nor anything else in all creation, will be able to separate us from the love of God that is in Christ Jesus our Lord. -Romans 8:39

Here are a few scriptures to strengthen you in this season

Zechariah 1:3, Ezekiel 36:26–37, Ephesians 4:24, Philippians 4:8, Jeremiah 17:7–8, Psalm 51, Colossians 2:6–7.

Father, thank You for the work my sister has done in Your name and for Your glory. Heal her heart from the wounds she's gained in service. Lord, harden not her heart—she desires to love like You, even when it hurts. Help her see it's okay to rest, to step back, to trust that what You started, You will finish.

Restore the joy of her salvation. Refresh her spirit. Restore her hope where it's been dry. Cause an overflow. Remind her that her best days are still ahead. Give her grace to release what she can't control. Shape, mold, and strengthen her for the next season. Let her be steadfast and immovable, setting her face like flint toward You.

We come against bitterness, frustration, and lack in Jesus' name. Help her fall in love with You again and remain in Your presence. Thank You, Lord, that we can come to You again and again and again. Amen.

My beautiful sis, keep growing. Keep becoming. Keep sitting with Him—because the best version of you is waiting in His presence.

What's Next?

Honestly, I'm not sure what's next, but we'll take it one step at a time. Whatever comes, I'll be ready—and I hope you will be too. If you'd like to stay connected, visit my website: *www.strivingforhisexcellence.com*.

Remember: You are Loved and You are Needed

–Yasmin Asante

MY THOUGHTS